PENNY A JAR

Keith Harris

FINELEAF
Ross on Wye
www.fineleaf.co.uk

First published 2010

ISBN 978 0 9557577 7 8

Design: Philip Gray
Typeface: Bembo
Print: SS Media Ltd
FSC Forest Stewardship Council certified paper

Images courtesy of The Changing Face of Bristol - www.gertlushonlineco.uk

Published by Fineleaf Editions, 2010
Moss Cottage, Pontshill, Ross-on-Wye HR9 5TB
www.fineleaf.co.uk books@fineleaf.co.uk

British Library Cataloguing in Publication Data
A catalogue record for this book is available from the British Library.

PENNY A JAR

1

Where to Begin

My memory transports me back to the years following the 1940's. Being a mere five years old at the time, the years prior to this are obscured. The war is well into its momentum and one night, like many others, my parents, brothers and sisters are all crammed under the stairs: how we managed to breathe I will never know. The aircraft above were getting louder by the second as they flew over the city of Bristol and the BAC - Bristol Aeroplane Company - site. I think we were more scared of my father than the anti-aircraft gunfire and the German planes flying above, as he kept on shouting at us to stop crying.

I don't remember falling asleep, just waking up at dawn and then trying to squeeze myself out from underneath our make shift air raid shelter. It was good to see the house still in one piece, or at least the inside where my grandfather is still sitting in his favourite armchair by the range, keeping it topped up with logs. He preferred to stay where he was despite the air raids. I got on well with him, better than with my father, even though he had a habit of poking his tongue out at me as I used to follow him around everywhere.

My grandfather's house was basic but in a good location, although the sanitation was a bit scary, having to journey down the garden night or day and in all weathers. I wasn't sure why we were staying with him at this time, but I guess it had something to do with the War.

Today is Sunday and a lovely day it is too; it is difficult to believe there is a war on, I'm visiting the scary toilet facility at the moment and dreading it. Inside the lean-to shed there is a long trench with a piece of rough timber over it, and the smell is breathtaking. A favourite pastime for some children in the village was to get into garden shed toilets and saw through the seating planks from underneath; you can guess the rest!

Beyond the back garden toilet there was a high hedge, and a gate leading out to a large meadow where I spent most of my free time while staying with my grandfather. My two brothers being a few years older had built a tree den made from a large piece of plywood and an old coconut mat they acquired from my grandmother. My brothers used to bully me a bit and would not allow me into their den, but secretly I used to venture up the tree when they weren't around. The den contained all sorts of junk which in those days we called our 'treasures', including apples scrumped from a local orchard. With my brothers up in their tree den in the afternoon my grandfather went to the top of the meadow along the hedgerow hunting for rabbits. He and my father did this quite often as this was about the only time we had meat with our dinner, but I used to cry when my brothers told me how my father killed them.

There is a saying that 'one can at times hear the silence'. That silence changed suddenly one day as out of nowhere appeared a number of fighter aircraft from above. I ran quickly towards the nearest safe area - my brothers' den in the tree, not that it would save us. I can still picture my grandfather running towards us, also hoping to climb into the tree den, but my brothers said no to us both as it wouldn't be strong enough. By the time we had both run to the back gate of the house my grandfather had an accident in his trousers, but my brothers thought it to be quite funny. I was told later that one of the fighter planes had been shot down in the field beyond the meadow. Unfortunately the police and air raid wardens told us we weren't allowed over there.

Today is Monday and it's back to school after a frightening but exciting weekend. My mother has walked me to school everyday since I recently started, and we arrive at the top of the lane only to be confronted by group of armed soldiers behind a barrier of barbed wire. I guess they have to check all grown-ups as we lived in quite a strategic area as far as the enemy was concerned. I recall a sign on the barrier stating 'Careless Talk Costs Lives'. This checking procedure continued for many months.

One afternoon, on the way home from school, I saw a lorry that had crashed by the barrier right through the railway bridge wall onto the railway. Fortunately the driver was okay but to our delight its whole cargo was liquorice allsorts, and all the packets and boxes had spilled over the tracks: talk about school is out! I think there must have been hundreds of us kids there, but the police stopped us going down onto the tracks. Most of the sweets were still there the next day, but it had been raining all night so that was the end of that.

My memories are a bit sketchy concerning the following few months. We finally moved to Tockington, about ten miles away, near a quiet village and to a house that had similar facilities to my grandfather's home, I remember we would collect our water from a huge cast iron pump which had to be primed before use. During the summer we had great fun with this pump, as it had a trough that children would sit in while others manned the pump handle.

Down at the bottom of our lane there was a beautiful watermill, which is where I spent most of my summer school holidays and many of my weekends. Money in my house for whatever reason was always very limited and many a night I would go to bed hungry. Thankfully, living in the countryside there were many orchards on the way to school and I would often turn up to class with my pockets stuffed full of apples, I consequently received a good few smacks of the ruler from my teacher for stealing, and for eating them during lessons and prayers.

The nearest village to us was about a mile away. My brothers and I would look forward to Friday evenings when my father would take us to the village pub, where he bought each of us a packet of crisps and a bottle of lemonade. It was a great weekly occasion, only spoilt by us not knowing if my father would reappear drunk from the pub. Some Friday nights he'd be fine, and he would carry me on his shoulders all the way home. I used to love it as he was a tall man, and I thought it so clever that I could look over the drystone walls that seemed to go on forever, especially on a moonlit night.

Moving further away from my grandfather's house made little difference regarding the air raids as we were still living fairly near the enemies strategic targets. Many a night was spent in an Anderson Shelter, which was less claustrophobic than being under the stairs,. Some nights, however, it would be flooded, so we had to take our chances indoors. I believe the bases of these shelters were supposed to have a kind of mastic base or tar to prevent water seeping in. Unfortunately many families could not afford to do this, even though the shelters came free. I spent many hours after school trying to bail out gallons of water using an old jam tin which seemed to go on forever. I would eventually come to tears as my brothers had left me to it.

At the age of five I think I only understood what was immediately around me, and all seemed well. The next few years proved to be a lot more revealing, as I started to realise I was living in some sort of family breakdown or domestic situation. One good thing I can remember about my father is that he was a hard worker, and his trade was bricklaying. He even used to travel into London to work, as anyone in the building trade was required to help with rebuilding after the bombs had fallen.

My mother was my best friend and she always tried to protect me in many ways but there was so much she kept from me regarding my father. I finally found out that he had lost his job for whatever reason, and he had even spent time in prison. Was this the beginning of the end for my family? To this day I never knew why my father was in prison but the following years took their toll.

Now, at the age of seven, we were in for another shock as we suddenly moved to a really old cottage on the edge of Tockington village. My brothers and I were very young and never had a clue about the family struggle going on around us. We just carried on in our own little world day by day and the old cottage became our latest adventure.

Why did we not have normal household facilities like lighting and water? In time all was revealed with great surprise and shock. As I said, my mother always tried to protect us, but it was a regular occurrence to find her crying in her quieter moments. This would scare me and would make me cry with her, I think we were quite close as we did so many things together.

The cottage as I remember could have been Victorian with its woodcarvings and wide staircase. Because of the lack of lighting, the banisters and landing shapes created an eerie vision, especially when the moon was peering through the skylight. Some nights I was too scared to go to bed, as my brothers would take advantage of the lack of light and would hide halfway up the staircase on the corner and jump out on me. If I screamed they used to drag me into the bedroom, put two pillows on my head and sit on me. The bed was quite small and all three of us had to sleep in it, you can imagine the rest. Whatever we were doing during our stay, we were constantly reminded of the war that was going on around us by the air raids, especially over Bristol. Some nights we would stay up for hours looking at the red sky in the distance over the city. There must have been many bombers over there as we could even hear the gunfire, especially from the famous gun battery at Purdown that was located quite close to us.

One night during a raid we could hear something happening nearby, so the next day we decided to investigate. To our surprise a barrage balloon had landed in the village square, having been blown to bits. I never quite understood why, but there was white powder everywhere. I guess to this day it was part of the balloon makeup; we thought it was so exciting at the time!

There are so many gaps in my memory of the stay in the cottage, but most of my memories are of being so very hungry. I was thankful for being in the country near so many orchards and potato fields. I used to walk through the fields for at least a mile just to find my favourite apples called Morgan Sweets: when I mention this variety, most people aren't aware of them. I don't remember my family ever sitting down together having a proper meal other than bread and jam, and occasionally some dripping which my mother managed to acquire from the local butcher. Rationing was well into operation but I don't remember my mother having ration books until much later.

Food was not the only thing in short supply. My clothes were worn through and shabby, the trousers I wore all had patches and holes in them and as I continued to grow that bit older I became very conscious of this, as my so called school mates used to call me all sorts of names, such as 'ragamuffin'. I hated that so much that I started playing truant and hid in fields all day until going home time,. My mother never had a clue that I was doing this, and I was dreading a visit from the school, which fortunately never happened. There was a good reason for this as the school never knew where I lived.

Our lives dramatically changed for the worst when the mystery was revealed regarding the cottage we lived in. It had apparently been condemned a number of years earlier and we must have been squatting there, but my father never explained to us why we came to be there. I knew there was a war on but now I noticed the lack of so many things such as food and money. Following this terrible revelation the family as I knew it collapsed and coming home one day after hiding in the fields I returned to an empty house, Where are my brothers? Where is my sister? Where's my mum? I don't remember asking for my dad as my mum was my best friend and was always there for us regardless of anything else going on.

As a family, we would live together again, but not before another period of the unknown for us all. During the last hours at the cottage I was lying at the top of the old staircase peeping through the banisters and eating an apple, which was one of three I still had stuffed in my coat pocket. While lying there I noticed how dirty I was, and well in need of a bath, which was something I hadn't had in such a long time - and my clothes weren't fit for a tramp.

To this day I don't know who the strangers were talking downstairs, but I remember hearing the word evacuation. I had heard the word before, but didn't realise they were using it talking about me, but about five minutes later I heard a lady's voice calling my name. She asked me to hurry down the stairs as it was turning dark in the cottage. I had a few of my secret treasures hidden away in a hole of my bedroom wall, but they said I had to go straight away - I wonder if they are still there?

I can't quite remember what kind of vehicle I climbed into, but it must have been some sort of small coach. There were other children on board and there was a tiny girl, I remember her because we were to cross swords at a later date! I remember looking back at the cottage and asking again where my mum was. I must have cried myself to sleep wondering where I was going, and would my mum be there to meet me?

After just a few miles I was awoken by an almighty bang as we reached Filton Village, which was a built up area and home to the Bristol Aeroplane Company. The driver parked up and turned the lights off as we had run into an air raid. Even to this day hearing sirens sends a chill straight through me and the frightful memories return. I tried to get comfortable but felt more hungry than scared. I remember peering into a grocery shop, looking at the tins of biscuits and Smiths crisps. I used to love unwrapping that little blue bag of salt, but maybe everything was fool's gold and the tins were probably empty due to the war. The grocery shop had this very large white faced clock just inside the door reading twenty minutes after midnight. I remember it well as an air raid warden knocked at the window and told the driver it was now safe to travel on. The momentum of the bus soon sent me to back to sleep, still not knowing where we were bound.

At the age of seven I had only ever visited the seaside once. I had heard of Weston Super Mare being next to the sea, and to my surprise that is where we arrived. For a short moment I forgot my fears, despite the blackout. I could just make out the white line of the tide coming in and back out, but at that moment I was unaware that we had arrived at our destination. It must have been around 2.30 am when we were shown into a tall building, possibly three floors high. We were met by, as I thought, two nurses who were quite firm with us. One of them implied that we could do with a good bath but as it was so late they just gave us some hot cocoa and put us to bed. The first thing I noticed was the wonderful white sheets and pillow cases, which were a rare luxury in my short lifetime. Even having a bed was a treat as my brothers were bullies and rarely let me share the only bed we had. I lay there for quite some time wondering how my mother was, and where she was. The little girl I mentioned was crying for her mum. I tried to console her by saying we could go to the beach the next day for a paddle, but we were abruptly told to shut up and go to sleep as we had a busy day ahead, I wondered for a while what she meant by that. Later that morning I was to learn that the nurses were not nurses at all.

The memory of that morning is so clear as we were woken to the music of The Trumpet Voluntary, which was coming in through the open windows from the direction of the beach. My view of the beach was somewhat restricted owing to the building being up a side street. To this day I would like to go back and look for it assuming it is still there, which is doubtful as it was already so old at the time.

Suddenly, the old creaky door to the room opened and there stood one of the nurses. She beckoned me and the little girl to follow her along an old corridor, the boards creaking with every step, which lead into a large dining area. I recall the smell of cooking was shear heaven as it had been such a long time since I had eaten a decent meal. There were many other children sitting on the long wooden benches, all whispering and laughing when they saw us. I was afraid to turn any other way but forward as my trousers had holes and patches at the back, and in those days underpants were a luxury.

All of a sudden you could have heard a pin drop as a nurse spoke very abruptly, demanding peace and quiet and ordered us to sit down. Looking along the wooden tables it appeared that most of the children had already finished their breakfast and I was wondering if there was anything left for us, but suddenly a bowl of porridge was placed in front of me followed by a plate of scrambled eggs. Despite my poor upbringing I knew how to say please and thank you so I said,'thank you for my breakfast nurse.' Immediately, the older girl next to me said, 'you silly bugger, that's a nun not a nurse'. At that moment I realised I was staying in a convent. I was so hungry I couldn't decide what to eat first. I decided on the scrambled eggs as they were my favourite of the two. When I started eating the porridge I thought someone was playing tricks on me as there was salt on it rather than sugar, this was new to me but I was quickly reminded by a nun that there was a war on and sugar was in short supply.

As I was finishing my breakfast I remember looking down at my dirty filthy legs and rags for clothes, wondering what was going to happen to me next. Suddenly a nun told me to take my empty plate and dish to the washing bin, as they called it, and follow her again down the creaky corridor. Some other children passed by and started laughing, I guessed that they were talking about the way I looked. My mother used to comment that children can be so cruel to each other at times. As we reached the far end of the corridor I was hit with the strong smell of disinfectant and I could hear the sound of running water. We entered a large tiled room. There was a row of baths with just one bath filled, so I guessed that it was for me, which it was.

The nun shut the door behind me and there in the middle of the room stood a very large lady dressed in a rubbery looking apron. When I think back now the scene reminds me of something from Oliver Twist. She immediately told me to get undressed, which I did, folding my clothes and placed them in the driest spot I could find.

'Don't bother with that,' she cried out loud. 'They are going on a bonfire, shoes and all.'

I was not used to being bathed by a stranger, but remember her really scrubbing me until I felt raw, and I remember the large bar of green soap she was using, which I think my mother also used for washing. After the bath I thought that was it, but she sat me naked on a stool and started to cut off all my hair. I could feel tears running down my cheeks just thinking what the other children will do or say when they see me, but the lady abruptly told me to stop crying as she was cutting it all off because I was lousy. After that she washed my head in a very strong smelling soap that I think was called 'Durback', and this was to be used on me many more times in the future. An hour or so had passed and I was led still naked into another room where there were plenty of clothes. She managed to fit me out including underpants, which I had never possessed in the whole of my short life before. My tears seemed to have disappeared as I was so happy about my new clothes, even if my underpants were actually girls knickers, which I only realised the first time I went to use the toilet.

Time passed so quickly that first morning that before I realised it, the wonderful cooking smell of something like cottage pie was spreading down the corridor again. It felt so good inside to know that I was actually going to have something to eat on a regular basis. Not long after that a loud bell sounded. Other children appeared from every direction, forming a single line along the corridor. Outside the dining room stood a very tall nun inspecting all of our hands. As for mine, they had only just been washed near down to the bone, so there was no problem there! Eventually we were all stood by the tables, but we were not allowed to sit until we joined the nuns in prayer. With both of my hands together I opened my eyes slightly and surveyed the rest of the children and the nuns. The nuns looked so serious which confused me a bit as I always thought that anyone to do with Jesus should always be smiling, but this was not always the case as I was to discover more so at a later date.

The little girl I arrived with was for some reason sat next to me, which continued throughout my stay at the convent. Teatime soon came around and we went through the same procedure again before we could eat. The main item we had was cheese and for what ever reason the cheese given to us was always hard, cracked, and yellow. Because I was always hungry I ate it regardless of feeling sick at times, the little girl next to me was the only one to mention my haircut and I reacted by telling her she looked skinny like Olive Oil in Popeye: she was to have her revenge the next day.

We had to be settled into our beds early that evening. For me this was not a problem because it was so wonderful to have my own bed and to experience clean white sheets, and no brothers to bully me or sit on me. I ought to have been too tired but I lay there for ages still wondering where my mum and family were, whispering to my new found bed pals. Suddenly the noise of aircraft came over reminding me why I was there, but fortunately it must have been the RAF as there were no sirens.

The next morning was a lovely start to the day. With the sun shining it was difficult to believe there was a war going on. The same music as yesterday was playing on the pier. Two of the nuns escorted a dozen or so of us to the beach. I couldn't remember ever going to a proper seaside resort before except for a trip to Severn Beach, which was not too far from my last home. Later I was to make many trips there. The beach was a short distance away and it was wonderful to walk and feel the warm sand under my feet. I clung on to my shoes like gold as I hadn't had shoes without holes in for such a long time. It was a wonderful feeling to wear something decent, and having no holes or patches in my trousers was great. I was still sore from the scrubbing I had been given the day before and was reminded quickly of it when my legs and feet came in contact with the salty water. Some of us walked out quite a way but we were abruptly beckoned back by one of the nuns. She explained that it was too dangerous for paddling any further out.

There were many other grown ups and children on the beach. Some were staring at us, and others were laughing and pointing. Later in life I was to discover that this was quite common where evacuees were concerned. The tide was far out and along the sands came an ice cream man on his bike shouting 'stop me and buy one!' A cone was only tuppence, but there was little chance of buying one, money was non-existent in my situation.

We left the beach after about two hours, by which time it was nearly lunchtime and I was already hungry again. I had spent so much time being short of food in the past that whatever it was for dinner, I never cared. When I got back I went straight back to my bed to see if it was still there - how silly! I loved it so much, it was still there, and all was well. Suddenly all hell broke loose as the dinner bell was going and the air raid sirens piped up at the same time. We were all rushed down to what looked like a large cellar, with the smell of dinner lingering down the stairs making me feel even more hungry.

This was my first experience of wearing a gasmask, which was quite frightening. At first I could hardly breathe, but I learnt to put up with it eventually. We did have a bit of fun with them too as we could make rude noises with them. The all clear sounded, but first we had to take our gasmasks back to our bedside cabinets, and then line up for lunch. The dinner I recall that day was mashed potatoes and beans. Some days we had an apple after our dinner but we had cold semolina that day. I ate it, but hated it.

In the afternoon, one of the friendlier nuns sat on my bed with me and asked me how far I had got in school with my lessons, mainly arithmetic. I was afraid to tell her that I spent much of my early schooling playing truant. However, she arranged for me to start some lessons the next day. The convent was where I learnt all my tables, reading and writing. During the months there I felt so different in so many ways. Apart from missing my mum I was quite happy to stay there.

That afternoon was the first time I got into trouble with a nun and saw the other side of her nature. Later in life, I would understand her reasons but at the time I thought her to be so cruel as the punishment to come was the sort of thing my brothers would inflict on me. The discipline I was to receive was entirely justified as while we had our hands raised to pray I peered down at my tea plate to see a horrible looking piece of cracked and sweaty looking cheese lying there, I looked around, and thinking no one else had their eyes open I reached down with one hand and threw the cheese under the table. That way I thought no one would know whose cheese it was.

Ten minutes into teatime it was spotted by one of the nuns, despite me pushing it further away with my feet. She immediately demanded to know whose it was. I said nothing, but she said no one would have any more to eat until the guilty person owned up. We all looked at each other and finally my little girlfriend told her it was me: as I said, she was to have her revenge and that was the day. The nun rushed around the table and grabbed me by the collar, pulling me down onto the floor. She ordered me to pick it up, but as I had pushed the cheese further underneath I had to crawl right under the table. The nun asked me to hand the cheese to her, and I thought she was going to dispose of it, but she told me to stay where I was, putting one of her hands behind my head and with the cheese in the palm of her other hand she pushed the whole piece into my mouth. I thought I was going to choke to death. She told me that there was a war on and hoped this would teach me a lesson. After that experience I always ate my cheese and to this day I am still quite fond of it.

I can't recall exactly how long, but I know I spent many months living at the convent. I think the experience has only been good for me, but obviously a good happy home would have been better.

2

Homeward Bound

The next part of my life is quite a sketchy memory as I don't recall much about my departure from the convent. I found myself reunited with all my family, in a semi-detached house located in Filton, and once again we were not far from military locations. We seemed to have moved in a complete circle. My father was in work again, my brothers were there too, as well as my older sister, and it all looked quite promising. Unfortunately the security I experienced at the convent had soon gone forever. My fears soon returned and I was wishing I could go back there.

Because of our past domestic situation there was very little furniture or standard requirements in the house. My brothers and I were to share a double bed, and on the very first night they threw me out just like old times and I ended up sleeping with just a blanket on the floor. They said that I should go back to where I had come from if I didn't like it. I was to sleep like this for many years to come. Gone was the proper bedding, white sheets and my nightly bath I had got used to at the convent. I find it so traumatic to even put this in writing as it's unbelievable how a family can end up in such desperation. I could just cry when I think about it.

Eventually I started school again and had an advantage over most of my classmates as I knew all my tables, which I owe to the convent. Because my father was working, the food situation had improved to what it had been previously in Tockington. There were still periods of shortages at times, pocket money was non-existent and this is when my own little ventures created my future income. To this day, I will never understand how my mother coped, looking after us throughout those difficult years. I realise there were thousands of people in the same situation during the war, and there were so many family breakdowns, but I never understood at that age. My mother would make a meal out of anything and always put us children first. Fridays were still our best day as my father used to get paid and we all had a bath bun from our local grocery shop. I always went shopping with my mum whenever I was allowed and she once again became my best friend.

This was the first time I saw my mum with ration books. I remember standing behind her in the grocer's many times when she was practically begging for extra rations, as these were sometimes available. When ration books were handed to the shopkeeper they would either cut tokens out or mark parts of the page with a pencil. As you can imagine, this was open to abuse as some people were desperate enough to rub the pencil marks out just to get extra rations. I recall my mum being accused of it one day but I can't imagine her ever doing that. I had an idea who might have, but was too scared to say anything - guess who?

I always loved gardening and had ideas of working in a nursery when I left school. In the meantime I started cultivating our back garden which was very long and wide. By the next season I was producing potatoes, vegetables and even strawberries. This helped my mum a great deal.

It was only a matter of time before the happy home I hoped for was no longer to be. There was always tension and my father, for whatever reason, started to drink again. Worst of all, he was drinking rough cider which was lethal. Being in the building trade he worked some Saturday mornings until noon, and would then go straight to the pub. My mum had his lunch ready, expecting him home, but it was mid-afternoon before he often appeared the worse for wear. If we were there we were all afraid to speak. Despite the war going on my father only liked to smoke Stars or Woodbines, which were in short supply. Unless you were extra friendly with your local tobacconist, the only cigarettes nearly always available were Turkish ones, known as Pasha.

One Saturday afternoon my father scrounged some fag money from my mum, and he told me to go up the paper shop to get him some cigarettes and a newspaper called The Green Un, which held the football pool results for that day.

'Dad, I think they have sold out of your cigs as I was there this morning,' I immediately replied.

He told me not to answer back and to do as I was told, and not to come back without his cigarettes. I was terrified, and was praying all the way to the shop that they would have had some come in. To my despair all they had were Turkish. I bought his paper and stood outside the shop for ages wondering what to do. Eventually I bought the Turkish cigs as he may not have any cigarettes at all and that would be just as bad. I remember running all the way home as I had already been gone an hour at least.

'Where have you been then?' my father cried, as I stepped in the front door.

My mum spotted the cigs in my hand and immediately stood between my father and myself as she knew what was going to happen. He grabbed the cigs with anger as mum told me to get upstairs for a while out of his way. Again my thoughts went back to the convent and wished that I was still there, even though it was very strict.

'Oh God, what am I doing back here?' I cried. 'There is nothing here for me.'

. . . .

Winter was upon us. Most days we had no heating in the house, apart from logs we collected locally by cutting down trees. We could not afford regular coal deliveries, but my mum found five shillings to buy an occasional bag of coal, which could be picked up on a Saturday from the local yard. All the coal delivery companies were located along a railway siding at Filton Rail Junction, about half a mile from my home,. We would collect the coal in an old pram from our coalman. On the way out we would pick up bits of fallen coal from the rail trucks, although there was a watchman at the gate who sometimes made us take the extra coal back. I don't know how, but one day we had a coal delivery. Because coal, like so many things, was rationed my father decided to have it tipped in the bath for safety.

To this day, I can never recall having a bath in that house. I gradually returned to being the scruffy urchin I used to be. I was even sent home from my new school within a month of starting because of nits in my hair. This happened quite often and my father used to cut all my hair off and my mum would scrub my head with the dreaded Durback soap. For different reasons I gave my oldest son Michael a haircut in his youth and never realised how devastated he was at the time. For that I am sincerely sorry, I hope he can forgive me.

At times, I look back and wonder if I did right by my own children and hope that I haven't been too unkind, as while fulfilling a parent's commitment one can be too busy working and lose the plot. I hope not. Michael bought me a CD by Mike and the Mechanics called *You can listen as well as you can hear:* so true, and thank you Michael.

Despite still being quite young and realising there was a better standard of living regardless of the war, I think I became a bit resentful of the way we lived. I became a bit distant and did my own thing, which I think made my father more aggressive to me and led to many beatings with his leather belt. When I look back, the discipline was deserved - but not the terrible welts on my body and legs.

One summer afternoon I, and other boys, lit a fire in our den in the lower lane behind the house. Accidentally, the fire spread to the railway bank and nearly set fire to the above telegraph wires. The railway station porter ran down the railway line, came down to us in anger and smacked us across our faces. That was bad enough but during the evening the station master came down and told my father what we had done. That evening I shall never forget because within five minutes of the station master leaving, my father rushed down the garden where my pals and I were playing, pulling his belt off as he came with my mum behind him begging him not to touch me. I fell to the ground with fear as my pals ran away.

'Please don't hit me Dad,' as I grabbed his legs as though to cuddle him.

This was the worst beating I can ever remember as he turned the belt to the buckle end, and beat me all over my legs. The buckle marks I can still remember to this day. Throughout my life I have always hated bullying in any form. Perhaps this had something to do with it, I don't know.

During the next few months the air raids intensified night after night. The standard of life in the house did not seem to matter because all we did was to live and breathe the war. We never had an Anderson Shelter like many neighbours in the street, and took our chances. Next door they had an indoor shelter in the form of a dinning table that the whole family could hide under.

Apart from the obvious strategic enemy targets around us, there was a very large rail complex immediately above the garden bank. There were many lines, including routes to London, Wales and Avonmouth, that being the main line to our most important dock. I suppose we should have considered ourselves lucky as there were so many people being killed in Bristol, but at that age we lacked reason and proper understanding.

The next few days we were to experience the true horrors of the death and destruction in the city of Bristol. I don't recall the build up to this, but I remember being on a bus one dark evening with my mum and dad. We were travelling down Gloucester Road towards the Bristol city centre. It was very scary as I could hear very loud bangs, and the bus driver could hardly see the road in front because of the smoke. There were many children on the bus and most were crying. At the road junction known as Stokes Croft the bus came to a sudden halt. Apparently a building had been hit by a bomb and the whole building had fallen across the road. We all got out of the bus as it was not going anywhere. Smoke and steam was still coming out from the hot debris and fire wardens were clambering over it hoping to find someone alive. There were people in dressing gowns and overcoats, and it was absolute chaos with everybody looking so confused. We were there for at least two hours and finally my dad and mum decided to carry on to our destination - but I had no idea what was in store for us.

Dad grabbed me by the hand and started to climb over the debris with mum following behind. The bricks were still hot.

'You can't do that,' shouted a loud voice.

Dad ignored the warden and dragged me down the other side, and my mum tore the only pair of stockings she had. Even clothes were rationed then. Her knee was bleeding and covered in sooty marks. I can remember that moment so clear to this day - God bless her.

Bombs were still falling but we still carried on down towards the city centre tripping over bricks and rubble everywhere. There were puddles and so much black mud around caused by fire hoses. We travelled through the centre and then along the riverside past the area where the SS Great Britain is in dry dock to this day. We eventually turned a corner and there in the darkness I saw the Bristol Suspension Bridge for the first time. I don't know if it was smoke or cloud but I could only see the outline of the structure.

'Do we have to climb up there Dad?' I asked.

'Be quiet!' was the reply.

It was so dark along the road that we could hardly see a thing, then all of sudden the air raid sirens started and that was when I became aware of the large number of people who were all around us. Some started running, which was the worst thing to do in the dark. Within fifteen minutes we had the all clear siren which allowed a bit of light to see where we were going, and eventually we passed under the bridge. There on the right of me were two very large doorways leading into a huge cave. It was frightening, and I remember clinging on to my mum's hand so tight and asking if we could go home.

The cave was massive and there must have been hundreds of people there. The water was constantly dripping through the cave ceiling and there were makeshift beds and mattresses all along the sides of the cave walls. I was quite hungry but mostly tired and fell asleep on a very damp mattress. I had no idea what time it was but woke suddenly as I had rolled off my bed and one of my arms was submerged in water. I cuddled up to my mum and tried to go back to sleep but realised there was a raid going on because I could hear sounds like bombs dropping and tiny rocks were falling from above.

Dawn arrived with a lovely sunny morning, and the situation we were in seemed to be less traumatic. I could smell cocoa and something cooking, and I guessed the ladies from The Women's Voluntary Service were nearby. An air raid warden came in and told us that Bristol had been badly bombed and a number of them fell locally including directly on top of us. We were to spend many more nights there, but eventually returned home to Filton to find our home still in one piece. There had been many raids in the area but we were lucky. I wonder if it was worth all that fear and anguish - I wonder.

3

All Clear

All clear is hardly a description to describe the ongoing trauma in my household, but I refer to a period of lull in the bombing raids. For quite sometime we all got on with living despite many difficult moments. I got settled in school again and made new friends. They were Welsh lads called Brian and Kenneth. Brian was epileptic, and I was to save his life more than once in the future. I never knew how to take their dad, but their mum was smashing. I got on well with her and spent a great deal of time with the family: she even let me have a bath there even though it was the same water as her boys used. I loved it.

I kept myself clean and tidy as well as I could, and even bought clothes from a jumble sale. My mum used to laugh at me as I used to rush through all the women at the sale to be first at the stalls, where I could pick up a pair of trousers for three pence. Food was still very short but despite that, my friend's mum used to feed me at times. Her husband had a regular job at the BAC, so I guess they were a bit better off than we were. Saying that however, in every street around us there were at least two large bins of waste vegetables for the 'pig man'. This was a life saver for some as people would raid them at night looking for anything useful. Even my friend's mother would remove wasted cabbage leaves. It sounds disgusting, but it happened.

We still had cabbages and potatoes in the garden, which I grew, and some Sundays we would have a proper dinner. Some weeks we seemed to be better off and my mum would buy a joint of meat for five shillings, and it was lovely. One of our treats on these Sunday meals was to wait for mum to strain the cooked cabbage, some of which she used for gravy stock and the rest she shared out between us to drink. Sunday teatime was a further treat as we had the dripping from the beef on our bread, and in those days there were no sliced loaves, so the pieces were like doorsteps as we called them. Lovely!

Some days we would have condensed milk or just jam on our bread until the Friday, when mum would get the rations again. My father started rabbiting with his ferrets and caught a few to help our food situation. Some days we never had enough to eat and my friends and I would go scrumping when possible. One day we came across an army camp that looked like something out of The Great Escape. Being young we were a bit scared as we thought that the men behind the barbed wire might be Germans. I remember the smell of cooking wafting through the barbed wire as we moved closer.

Suddenly, two of the soldiers, dressed in dirty grey uniforms, came close to fence. They spoke to us in broken English and introduced themselves, asking us our names. I whispered to my friend Brian not to tell them as we were taught that careless talk costs lives!

'I think you hungry,' one of the soldiers said with a smile.

He turned around and walked into a nearby hut, returning with two hot meat pies. We managed to get them through the wire and immediately someone dressed in all white clothing shouted, and the soldiers went back into the hut which we found out later to be the camp cookhouse.

We were to learn later that the soldiers behind the fence were Polish, and we were to visit the camp many times over the next couple of years. We made great friends with them, not to speak of the goodies we enjoyed. We kept our visits quiet as both our parents disapproved.

The long hot summers were wonderful and my friend Brian, his brother and I were to have great adventures in so many ways. We hadn't a care in the world. During the eight weeks of school holiday my parents hardly saw me from morning to dark: for me it was a happier world outside.

I would occasionally hear other children talk about pocket money, but that was unknown in my household, although I know my mum would have given us money if she had it to spare. I was always stealing apples, especially when I was hungry. We had our favourite orchards and apples and took it as a normal thing kids did, never thinking of it as stealing. I only got caught twice, once by a farmer and the other was at a private house. The owner must have known I would arrive there just after school, so he hid inside the hedge and grabbed me by the neck as I climbed in.

'Got you, you little basket,' he said.

I immediately wet myself with fright and he started laughing.

'Hope that has taught you a lesson, and next time I will call the Police.'

As you can imagine I never went back there again, but out of necessity I continued scrumping.

My father would sometimes use The George public house on a Saturday night. I would climb on to the pub window ledge to see if I could see him, hoping he would buy us a packet of Smith's crisps. One Saturday evening we decided to do something really dishonest by climbing over the pub fence to steal the empty beer bottles and return them to the 'Bottle and Jug' as it was called in those days. Stealing apples was one thing but doing this I felt really guilty and scared. We did it a few times over following months but I think the landlady started to suspect something. From then on, any money I had was honestly earned and earned, which brings me to my first attempt to create my own source of pocket money.

There was a grocery shop called Moody's about a mile away and they paid money for empty jam jars. They were paying a penny for the two pound jars and half a penny for the one pound jars. We immediately started looking in ash bins in all the streets, especially on bin day. Most people said it was alright, but some of the better off people told us to push off. My mother was always genteel, and never swore, but she had a saying about those sort of people; she claimed they forget they have a backside too.

Summer was upon us and it was break-up time at school, for eight long weeks. We started our business venture straight away, raiding the street bins and collecting about sixty mixed jars on the very first day. The summer days were long and we spent the evening washing the jars in our local pond as most of them still had bits of jam in them, not to speak of an occasional wasp or two.

The next morning was warm and sunny and I was up and out of the door to find my friend Kenneth, Brian's brother, waiting for me. We collected our jars from our hiding place and made off to Moody's. We had to queue behind several ladies but eventually we got to the front, we were quite excited as the shopkeeper gave us five shillings which was a fortune to us. Mr. Moody told us that we could bring jars to him at any time in the future, which inspired us to carry on with the search for more jars. Apart from bin days it was a bit more difficult to collect them and we were chased out of many gardens.

Having money in my pocket, one of the first things I bought was a Penguin bar for two pence. These were the only choc-bars not on ration, and that left me with two shillings and four pence. I felt so good. The war was still going on, with air raids mainly over Bristol, but somehow it never bothered me quite so much. Perhaps coming up to my tenth birthday I was older and less scared. My parents and brothers at this time never knew about my money making, and I managed to keep it quiet for sometime. I kept my money hidden in the back garden in a tobacco tin that my grandfather had given me.

One bin day we realised that so many jars still ended up in the ash man's lorry, so we decided to find out where he tipped his load. It was in Patchway, near where I used to live, about two miles across the fields behind where I was living. We soon decided to make the trip to the rubbish tip to collect more jars. We had to be careful as we had to go over two railway lines which was forbidden, and patrolled by rail police and the army. Brian, who suffered with fits, decided to fish at a local pond on the way to the tip, so Ken and I decided to continue on our own and leave Brian to it. After walking a few yards I turned around and shouted to Brian to suggest that we all did the fishing on the way back as I remembered his mum telling me not to leave him on his own. All of a sudden there was this almighty splash. We called Brian but with no reply. We ran back to the pond to see him slide below the water level. I can still see him now with his eyes wide open, his eyelashes trembling and the whites of his eyes staring upwards. The pond was very deep and neither of us could swim. I was terrified, but took a deep breath and jumped in. Fortunately it was not in the middle and I was able to stand with the water up to my chin. I grabbed Brian by his jacket's lapel and pulled him towards the shallower edge of the pond. As I took some of his weight I sank a bit, and took in a mouthful of dirty green water. To this day I can still see the grey fleck jacket he was wearing as he lay on the side of the pond. Ken grabbed my hand and helped me climb out, then together we dragged Brian out on to the grass. Being wet and limp he was very heavy.

We had no idea what to do but I remembered seeing a fireman turn someone on their side during a bombing in Bristol and thought we would try that, which we did. We continued calling and shaking him at the same time. We were both in tears and hoped we were doing the right thing.

All of a sudden, Brian came round and started coughing up water, I don't think he had any idea of what had happened to him as the first thing he did was to give us a big smile as though embarrassed. We lay there in the hot sunshine for a further hour or so to dry out. Above us steam trains were rumbling by, which reminded us about the railway police who could appear at anytime. With that in mind we crept up the railway bank and went across several lines to the other side. I had to be extra careful as my house was nearby and we could have been seen from the kitchen window. Brian was feeling a bit weak so we rested for a while before eventually getting him home to his mum. We couldn't tell her everything as our parents had forbidden us to go on to the railways, especially my dad, as you know what happened to me before. I left Brian and Ken and made my way home looking worse for wear and disappointed that we never did make it to the tip.

My mum never noticed anything as I suppose she was used to seeing me looking scruffy. I asked her if she had been shopping as I was so hungry.

'Not until Friday,' she said.

Today was only Tuesday so I could see it was going to be a hungry few days ahead. Standing in the corner of the kitchen area was this large white metal food cabinet and on the front my dad had fitted a padlock. He held the only key, knowing that if mum held the key she would give whatever was in there to us children.

Mum did her best and cooked me egg and scallops, being chips of course. I used to think I got more if the potatoes were cut that way, normally if we were lucky in the mornings we would have Quaker Oats, but that morning I didn't have anything as I thought we would be able to scrump some apples on the way to the tip.

The next morning I went to my friends' house to see how Brian was and to re-plan our visit to the tip. Unfortunately he looked a bit worse for wear and he was kept indoors for the rest of the week. Ken had spent his jar money already so we planned to visit the tip on the following Sunday morning as it was less likely that the tip's caretaker would be there. For the next two days I knew there would be very little food in the house, so decided to retrieve my tobacco tin and buy some chips. My favourite treat was to buy a small loaf for four pence and a bag of chips for two pence, then empty out the loaf's dough and fill it with chips and plenty of vinegar. I can still smell and taste it to this day.

When I look back again to my past I can understand why I got a clip round the ear, or a hiding, as I must have been a handful; but beatings, no way. I can laugh when I think about it now, but one day when I was home on my own and feeling really hungry I climbed on the shelf behind the steel pantry and I discovered the pantry had a small square vent held by screws. I was able to unscrew them using a bread knife and put my arm right inside. I pulled out quite a big piece of cheese, cut a piece off and immediately replaced the vent.

I was shaking like a leaf in case my brothers or parents came home but enjoyed the cheese, which I ate with onions from my garden behind the shed. I was to repeat this secret procedure several times and would watch the look on my dad's face when he sat down to eat his cheese at teatime, sometimes he would look a bit confused, but he never said anything.

One Saturday night I was to be caught out. While my mum and dad were at the pub I told my brothers that I knew a way into the pantry if they were hungry. They were all for it, so I unscrewed the vent and put my hand inside to reach for the cheese, but stuck my hand into something soft. I managed to retrieve the cheese but to our disappointment all remained was a thick piece of hard skin. The three of us decided to go to bed before my parents arrived home, but within ten minutes of arriving home my father called us down and told us to sit at the table as he had something to show us. He immediately placed a dish on the table containing dripping.

'Since when did we have mice in the pantry?' he said.

He looked at me as I was smiling and near to laughing, mainly for what he said about the mice. He then reached for the cheese and I thought it was curtains for me, but he never said anything about it. Sometimes when my father had been drinking he would be in a good mood and fortunately this was one of those rare occasions. I think my mum had an idea of who the culprit was, but explained to my dad that she must have disturbed the dripping while it was still warm. With much relief I went to bed knowing what I put my hand in: being so hungry at times I would eat anything.

Sunday arrived and Ken was at my front door early. It was a glorious morning and we could already feel the sun on our backs. We made our way down the lane at the back of my house, as far away as possible so that my parents could not see me climb the railway bank. When we were on the railway we had to run for cover as there was a 'matchbox train' coming. These were used for all the shunting in the rail sidings. We hid behind a rail shed until it had gone by.

While we were waiting we noticed that the shed was unlocked, so we ventured in and discovered an open box of detonators under the seat bench. Apparently the rail gangers put these on the rail lines when there were foggy conditions. To this day I am not sure if this was for the benefit of the train driver or other rail personnel. The detonators were quite simple looking and shaped very much like a milk sachet, but flatter. The idea was to place them on the railway line and it would explode with a very loud bang as the train wheels ran over it. We decided to have a bit of fun and placed two of them on the line for the next train due then ran like mad down the bank, scratching and cutting my leg on the blackberry brambles. That served me right I suppose. I had second thoughts about the detonators and wanted to go back to remove them, but hearing a train coming, we just kept running.

We arrived at the next railway line and for a moment forgot about the detonators, as we climbed the embankment where we were taken aback by size of the tip that was before us. It was huge and for what we wanted: it was an Aladdin's cave just waiting to be discovered. Being Sunday there was no one around so we immediately scrambled down the bank towards it. The first thing we noticed was the awful smell, but we got used to it after a while. There were several small fires burning but that didn't stop us doing our hunting.

There were all sorts of handy bits and pieces lying around which we were to make good use of at a later date. We found plenty of jam jars, but concentrated on the larger ones as we knew they were worth more money. The wasps and flies were everywhere but we managed to avoid getting stung. We collected so many jars so quickly but we hadn't stopped to think how we were to get them to the shop.

By this time we were in the thick of all the rubbish and suddenly could hear the sound of a tractor getting louder. There was nowhere to run so we just lay down among the rubbish. There was a field beyond the tip with a hedgerow, but there was not enough time to run and hide. The engine we could hear stopped quickly and we could see a figure stood at the tip edge looking down. I guess it was the tip caretaker doing his rounds. All of a sudden he started shouting and I thought the game was up for us, but soon realised he was talking to his dog. I thought the dog was going to give us away as it started to come down into the tip towards us, wagging its tail in excitement. Thankfully the owner shouted at the dog again to come out of that dirty rubbish, and within five minutes they were gone.

We moved further around the tip and saw the answer to our problem of transporting our jars to the shop - empty orange boxes that were perfect for the job. The field beyond the tip was planted with sugar beet for the cattle. In the corner of the field was a pond located in a triangle between the two railway lines. This was perfect for us as we could store and clean our jars in the same place, and it was a safer access to the railway and the shop.

We decided to fill four orange boxes with jars and store them in a hedge next to the pond after we had cleaned them. We were carrying the first two boxes across the field when all of a sudden we heard two almighty bangs as though someone was firing a shot gun. We soon started to laugh as we realised it was our detonators going off.

We spent the next couple of hours washing and repacking the jars ready for the next trip to the shop, by which time we were getting very hungry as neither of us had eaten any breakfast that morning. I had a thought that if cattle ate the sugar beet, it can't be poison so surely we could eat it too. We pulled up and broke open one root, which was not easy, and took a bite. It was a bit bland but being so hungry we managed to eat quite a bit. While the sugar beet was there we were to eat them a few more times in the future.

It took us all morning the next day to deliver our jars as it was like running the gauntlet, trying to avoid the rail police and other children from finding out what we were doing. Our daring efforts paid off that day as we shared the money, and had earned ourselves two shillings and six pence each. This may seem like peanuts today but back then was a fortune; we were more than satisfied with what we had. I still had money in my tobacco tin and enjoyed my visits to the chip shop. Sometimes I could buy sweets off ration so I spoilt myself there as well.

I tried very hard to be discreet with my money but my brothers wanted to know what I was chewing when I had sweets, and one thing led to another. One night as we went to bed they got bored and decided to torment me, trying to find out who gave me the money. I could only tell them the truth but they continued to bully me by sticking two pillows over my face and sitting on me. It was more painful as I was sleeping on the solid floor, and I could hardly breath. I screamed out to get them off but they carried on regardless. Being on the floor, and the boards being bare, I banged the floor with my fist to attract my parents' attention. They immediately jumped back to their bed as though nothing had happened. This was to continue for the rest of the week, but they then dragged me on to their bed so that I was unable to alert anyone.

I think bullying was the cause of the nightmares I was to experience for a considerable time afterwards. The fear in my nightmare was first not wanting to close my eyes because I could see coins all around me, then each night the coins would increase until they touched my mouth and stopped me breathing. One night in my dreams my brothers dragged me down the road to a railway signal box, below which was a deep ditch and a tunnel leading under the bridge. They said there was a dead body hidden in the tunnel and I had something to do with it. I awoke screaming, and to this day I relive the dream every time I drive under that bridge at Filton Junction. Perhaps there is a body there?

My father was well known to be a bit handy with his fists and both my brothers were to follow him in that way. They joined a boxing club at an early age and in fact Ron eventually became the Bantam Weight Champion of West England. I don't recall Bill ever really hitting me but Ron would always spar up to me. Because I always turned away he would punch me on the arm or my side until I fell on the floor in agony. This is another reason I loath bullying in any shape or form. I recall one day seeing Ron tormenting a boy from across the street over a Mars bar. He was quite timid and handed over the chocolate to Ron. I can still recall him saying, 'you can have my Mars Bar, Ron,' as tears ran down his cheeks.

Although we said we would only go to the tip on Sundays, my friends and I decided to take a chance and go midweek as there were still plenty of jars to be had. After making our way over the railway lines we climbed down on to the tip. With no sign of the tip keeper we spent many hours there and collected loads. Washing them took most of the time, and when we felt a bit hungry we helped ourselves to more sugar beet. Brian of course had recovered and was with us again, providing we kept him away from the pond. We also had to avoid getting him excited as that is when he was most likely to have a fit. Ken and I were a bit worried as he was not used to having money in his pocket, but he reacted quite calmly when we shared the money out the next day.

Most of the jars we collected so far were at the base of tip, so on the following Sunday, and armed with sticks in the shape of hooks, we climbed the tip bank and started raking through the rubbish. We were soon to learn that there were areas for different types of rubbish and moved around a bit. Half way up the slope on our way around, I had a terrible shock as looking at me from the rubbish was this pair of piercing eyes. I screamed out to Ken and Brian that there was a dead body under the rubbish. I dropped my stick and practically fell down the tip slope, scratching my legs on the way. Immediately above me was a lorry tipping its rubbish and I called out to the driver, telling him what I saw, but he just laughed and said we should not be there and not to get caught by the tip man.

We were surprised to see a lorry there on a Sunday as we had assumed the tip was closed. After a while we acquired a bit of courage and climbed back up the tip to look for the dead body. I retrieved my stick and we proceeded to rake the rubbish away from around the big eyes that were still peering at us. The three of us were trembling as we uncovered the rest of the dead body, only to reveal it was a horse's head. Being an animal lover I was more upset than scared, I don't think there was any rules to what could be put into rubbish tips in those days. We were to find more horse heads each time we went, which was so sad. I once read the story Black Beauty but could never read it again to this day. I think, really loving animals is a wonderful gift to posses.

Over the next couple of weeks we were to make plenty of pennies. In fact, the shop keeper asked us to give him a break for a week as we were supplying him faster than he could get them collected from his storeroom. We carried on collecting and stored them in the field until he was ready again. Visiting the tip so often I noticed how many old bikes were thrown away, which gave me another money making idea. The three of us had a chat and decided to start collecting them to make up complete bikes, within reason, and then sell them. This was the beginning of another new venture and we eventually did quite well. Ken's mum was not too keen on the idea of having bits of bikes here and there, but she said at least it will keep us out of mischief. In my garden, I had as many as eight bikes that we were assembling at one time, some bikes took longer depending on the availability of parts.

We were selling the bikes for around three pounds ten shillings, and less for the ones that had no brakes or mudguards. These simpler bikes were quite common in those days as children would just use their feet to stop their bike by jamming their shoe between the front forks. I used to do it, but one day while riding down a country lane in Stapleton, my foot jammed in the forks and I did a complete summersault over the handlebars, landing in the ditch. The money we made on the bikes and jam jars may not sound a lot today, but it was a fortune to us at the time. We were to continue with our money making schemes for quite sometime with only a break during the winter.

We had two more weeks left before going back to school and out of the blue my mum said that my dad was going to take us all to the seaside. This was unbelievable as he had never taken us to a beach before, and where would he get the money from?

I got excited as I thought we might be going to Weston, and I could go to the convent to see if my little girl friend and others were still there. Even though it was quite strict, I was never beaten and that was the biggest difference for me. On many occasions I wished I was back there but this was not to be the case.

To my disappointment we were not bound for Weston but to Severn Beach, a place I had never been to. Apparently it was not a long journey but we had to catch two trains to get there. Finally the day arrived and it was hot sunny as we boarded the train at

Filton Junction heading for Pilning. There we would change for Severn Beach. The carriages were pulled by the 'matchbox train', and I remember all of the children pushing for a place at the carriage window to get the best view of the train in front. It was quite funny really as unknown to us, being so close to the engine, most of us ended up with black faces from the soot.

We arrived at Pilning and waiting in the sidings was another train, with only three carriages. When we all got on it reminded me of the *St. Trinians Train Robbery* film, with children hanging out everywhere. After a short while we arrived at Severn Beach and made our way to the front sea wall. I was disappointed in a way, as there was no comparison to Weston, but thought it great that my mum was with us and it was the first day out that I could ever remember having with the family.

There was no sand on the beach to speak of, but both my brothers wondered off leaving me to myself. I was quite pleased really as I was able to spend some of my money without being bullied. I had a couple of rides on the donkeys and palled up with the donkey owner's son. They invited me to come down any weekend during the summer if I wanted, and help with the walking of the ponies. Apart from free rides, this was even more fortunate as they lived in Filton, and would give me a lift there in their truck.

At lunchtime mum called us together as my father was going to take us to a pub on the green for lemonade and crisps. Everything was great and it was easy to forget that the war was still with us, with all the terrible things going on around the world. Many essential things like food were in very short supply, and today we were to experience the unpleasant side of my father once again as all the pub had to drink was rough cider. It was quite cheap and he never really disliked it, but it always got the better of him. We had our lemonade and crisps and lay in the hot sun for which seemed like hours waiting for him to come out. Eventually my mum had to get him out as we had to get the last train back to Filton. For the rest of the afternoon he was quite nasty and spoilt the whole day out. We arrived home late evening and were made to go straight to bed without any food. I could still hear him arguing with my mum late at night so I covered my ears with my blanket. This was the first time I had serious thoughts of leaving home, but how at my age? I had no idea.

The next morning I was awake early and just wanted to go out. I could hear my father downstairs getting ready for work, so I lay there on my makeshift bed until the front door shut. My brothers were quite happy to stay in bed much longer than I could: even to this day I am unable to do that unless I'm unwell. At the top of the landing we had a large mirror. On my way down I stopped and looked at myself, thinking how scruffy I looked and wished I could be back at the Convent.

Our bath still had coal in it so the only place to wash was in the kitchen sink. I hated it as the water was always cold, and mum used to use the same soap as she used for washing. It stung like mad especially if she scrubbed me too hard. This morning I endured this again before mum made me some porridge. I was so hungry as I had not eaten since lunchtime the day before. Later that morning I made a visit to our local grocery shop and bought some broken biscuits; the whole bag only cost tuppence.

The rest of the day I spent on my own wandering along the railway banks picking wild strawberries. It was quite hot and I could feel the sun burning my shoulders, so I decided to take cover by a nearby haystack and fell asleep for quite some time. I must have been over tired for some reason. To this day I have always loved wildlife, especially birds, and as I lay there so still there were pheasants pecking at the bits of corn close by and the sound of the crows to make my day. I felt so secure somehow and wasn't looking forward to going home. After a while, I decided to start making my way home, taking a shortcut across two railway lines. The second rail was a bit more difficult as there was a train waiting at the signals to move, so I took a gamble and climbed between the wheels of the trucks, I would never do a thing like that today.

It was about 5pm when I walked up my back garden and my mum opened the back door telling me my dinner was ready.

'Where have you been all day?' she shouted. 'Hurry up and eat your dinner before your father comes home.' To keep the peace, she never mentioned a word to him.

I spent the rest of the evening doing some weeding in my garden as due to collecting jars and bikes I had neglected my garden a little. The produce I grew helped my mum in the kitchen; cabbage, carrots, parsnips and even some strawberries. This again was where I made good use of jam jars as I used to train the strawberry foliage to grow into the jars, firstly to protect them from the birds and it also helped them to ripen quicker.

It was now getting dark after a most wonderful long summer day and my mum was calling me. I was so happy when I was outside especially when the sun was shining, and to this day I always call the sun 'my best friend'. Reluctantly, I went indoors, had a drink of cocoa and went to bed - and as always without a wash. Most of all I wanted a kiss or a cuddle, which was non existent in my household.

Even though the nuns were very strict at the Convent, we were tucked in with a smile most nights. Perhaps I was too young to understand at the time what love was, and in what form it came. I will always remember my mum saying that when poverty walks in, love walks out, or something similar to that.

4

Revelation

Being children in that era, I think we all understood to a degree the difficulties around us being caused by the war, but some families had deeper problems that were more difficult to cope with than others. Just one more day and it was to be my tenth birthday. I had remembered, but no one else had. I raided my hidden tobacco tin in the garden and made off to the sweet shop and to see my friends Brian and Ken. Their mum always seemed to be pleased to see me, and that day I had a nice bath after the boys finished. She even gave me a pair of trousers and a shirt as those I had on were torn and filthy. Because of Brian's condition, she was always pleased if he was with me when he went out. I suppose she trusted me to look after him somehow. Today felt like an early birthday as when I told her it was my birthday tomorrow she cut and washed my hair. I was so worried in a way as I knew I had lice, but she never said a word. I guess she could probably see I was embarrassed. She even made some iced cakes and let me stay to tea with the boys. I felt so clean and quite excited somehow with my new clothes until I got home when my father started shouting.

'Have you been telling your friends we are bloody poor?'

Couldn't he see how clean and tidy I was? I thought he would be pleased, especially as we were going back to school soon.

'You can bloody well stay away from your friends' house in future,' he cried.

My mum looked at me and quietly suggested I said nothing, I was afraid to say that I had already had my tea so sat at the table with my father sitting opposite.

'I'm still waiting for an answer,' he shouted.

'She told me to be quiet,' I said, looking at him.

The next thing I felt was his fist in my face knocking me and a full bottle of milk on to the floor at the same time.

'She is the cat's mother,' he shouted.

After that I was to suffer with regular nosebleeds for many years, I was told that it was quite the norm for some people to suffer from nosebleeds, so accepted it. At the age of eighteen in the Royal Air force it was discovered that I had a broken nose all those years.

Thankfully that evening my father went out and my mum took me to the pictures, which became quite a regular thing almost every week. I know my mum had little money so I never mentioned my birthday, but to my surprise that evening she told me she was taking me out the next day as a birthday treat.

'Where are we going Mum?' I said excitedly.

'It's a surprise,' she told me.

We arrived home about 10.30pm and my father, thankfully, was still out somewhere. Mum suggested I took my cocoa to bed before he came in, not knowing what mood he might be in. I went to bed straight away but it took me ages to go to sleep as my left jaw and my nose were starting to feel quite sore. During the night I had a nose bleed but managed to keep it secret as I didn't want to miss my day out with my mum.

Saturday arrived and it was my tenth birthday. Dad had gone to work for four hours and I was raring to go. Unfortunately my mum could not take me out until my father came home at lunchtime. 12.30 arrived and there was no sign of him.

'Let's go. I bet he's gone to the pub,' she said.

Still not knowing where we were going, we boarded the bus at Filton and changed onto another bus in Bristol. We ended up in Newfoundland Road where I was to discover I had a grandmother, an auntie and two uncles that I never knew about.

My grandmother was really lovely as she was so much like my mum. We got on so well and I was to visit her weekly for sometime. Each time I went we would have tea, homemade cakes and, best of all, toast with plum jam toasted on the grills of the huge range she had in the kitchen. The kitchen looked like something out of the Charles Dickens era and it felt so homely. Along the sidewall was a Victorian settee with scatter cushions of all colours. There was a brass log box next to the range, brightly polished, and even the poker handle was shining. I loved it so much there and a week seemed to be a lifetime before I would go again. Each visit, my grandmother insisted on giving me sixpence to go home with: money was short but she insisted.

It was well into the afternoon and my mum mentioned a visit to my aunt and uncle down the road when suddenly the air raid sirens started and the three of us jammed ourselves underneath the staircase. After twenty minutes we had the all clear. My mum took me to the front gate and proceeded to point to the house where my aunt and uncle lived.

At the time I never understood why my mum was not coming over with me; that was to be revealed later. I walked down the half-bombed street noticing many people, mainly women, sat on their doorsteps in the sunshine. On the other side of the road was a long stone wall separating the street from a river, which I think was the Frome. Even the wall itself showed shrapnel damage, and many of the headstones had fallen into the river below it. One of the old ladies called me away from the wall, telling me it was unsafe. I can picture her now. She was wearing a long black dress and had daps on her feet, or plimsolls as we call them now, and she had on a man's cap: I had never seen that before. I looked back up to where my gran lived and my mum was still at the gate beckoning me to hurry up. My aunt's door was open and in the hallway my aunt and uncle were talking, and wondering who the strange looking boy was at the door.

'It's Keith,' I shouted, and with that they came to the doorway and introduced themselves.

'Did you come all this way on your own?' my aunt asked.

'No, my mum brought me. Look she is standing at Gran's front gate.'

There was no response, and not even a wave to my mum as they beckoned me down the hallway to the kitchen. After having tea and cakes I returned to my gran's where my mum eagerly awaited my return to know how I had got on. After a lovely day out I felt reluctant to leave but had to say goodbye to my gran and board a bus for home.

After about five minutes the bus had to turn around as the police said there was an unexploded bomb in someone's front garden nearby. We were then diverted into the main part of Bristol before we could turn back in the direction of Gloucester Road. We eventually arrived at Sussex Place, which was the very location where we had climbed over newly bombed buildings only a few years before. It was at this point we were to change buses for Filton. Because of war disruption, bus timings were a bit erratic and sometimes they would drive straight past when they were completely full. We waited at least an hour and sat on the cinema steps behind us. It was the Academy and in later years to become a restaurant called the Yentella, which later closed down.

Our bus finally arrived, and like many children I wanted to travel upstairs at the front if possible. My mum reluctantly followed me and we managed to acquire a front seat. Even though we saw our share of war activities where we lived, the view from the upper deck of the bus was frightening and I was glad we never lived in the City.

As we pulled away from the bus stop I asked my mum why she never went to my aunt and uncle, but there was no reply. I looked up and tears were running down her cheeks, falling on to her lovely silk white blouse she always kept for something special. I didn't quite know what to say, so I just put my arm in hers and said thank you for my birthday treat, and I kept quiet for the rest of the journey home.

It was late afternoon when we arrived and all was quiet for a change. I immediately went to my money box in the garden and set off to see Brian and Ken to make plans for our visit to the tip tomorrow, and to see if we had a bike ready for sale. It was only two days since I had seen them but I missed them so much, being my best friends. After planning our next day and a visit to the chip shop, we spent the evening playing 'kick tin' with other kids until dark.

We planned to meet up very early the next morning, as we were hoping to make a double trip to the tip. Within a week or so we were due back to school, so weekdays would be much more difficult for trips there.

I arrived home about 9pm and my dad had gone to his local pub. My mum had cheered up a bit and we ended up having a bit of a laugh about certain things: we seemed to have the same sense of humour in some ways. Later I made my way upstairs to bed before my dad got home, just in case he was in the wrong mood. I lay in my bed for some time thinking about the day's events, and my mum's secret, then suddenly I heard my dad come in the front door so blew my candle out and pretended to be asleep.

The next morning I was awoken by the milkman rattling his bottles, and the sound of my dad's chickens in the back garden. It was a lovely sunny day and I was so eager to get out. The pantry door downstairs was padlocked as usual so there was no food to be had unless I woke my mum up. Rather than do that, I picked a few strawberries from my garden and made my way along the back lane to the main street.

'You're up early for a young boy,' someone shouted.

It was the milkman, peering at me from the side of his van.

'I could do with someone like you to help me on a Saturday mornings,' he said, and told me he would pay me two shillings and sixpence plus an extra free bottle of milk for my mum.

I agreed straight away and would work for him for the next two years or so. His name was Mr. Robinson and he was to have a large impact on my life over those years to come, leading to some of the happiest times. It was still quite early so I sat in his van until we reached my friend's street.

'See you next Saturday,' he said with a smile as he drove away.

It was about 7am and my friend's bedroom curtains were still drawn, so I decided to sit in their back garden and wait. Although it was quite early, the sun was shinning as it always seemed to back then. Some years we would have eight weeks of sunshine throughout the whole summer school holidays. It was wonderful.

Suddenly, the back door opened and Ken's mum called me to ask me if I had eaten breakfast. I said yes, but she knew I was lying and sat me down at their table for a bowl of porridge with golden syrup on it. My dad warned me not to accept anything from there but I was so hungry and never cared about that.

Very soon we set off down to the railway sidings to choose where we were going to cross the first railway line, but to our disappointment there were gangers working on the lines so we had to carry on walking quite a long way before we could safely cross without being seen. We came across a ganger's hut we had never been in before, so we sat inside for a while, the fire was alight so we guessed the gangers would be making tea there soon. Fate is a very strange thing, as I was to spend a night in the same hut and by the fireplace ten years later in freezing temperatures whilst in the Royal Air force.

We walked so far that morning that we ended up in Patchway, which was the main entrance to the tip. Through my own curiosity I climbed a bank which I had done so many times before at the age of four and five to see my old house, and where my brothers and I used to stand in the meadow watching the RAF fighting the enemy above without fear. Brian and Ken were a bit lost in that area but fortunately I knew a short cut to the tip, which would only take about fifteen minutes.

Brian and Ken joined me on top of the bank, where we sat for a while in the glorious sunshine: from there we could see the railway bank where some years before I recalled the incident about a lorry load of liquorice allsorts ending up on the railway lines. When I think back, it reminds me of one of my favourite stories, The Railway Children, which I love still to this day. We were poor, but so happy in those days somehow. Why did growing up seem to spoil everything?

After a while we clambered down the bank and proceeded in the direction of the tip towards Patchway railway station. It was here where my brothers' guardian angels were to be with them in the earlier days of the war. One afternoon, they were walking towards the station, when suddenly out of nowhere came a German fighter plane, the pilot must have seen them and proceeded to fly lower towards the road firing his machine gun. They reached the station just in time as bullets hit the walls just missing them by inches. We ran our fingers through the bullet marks and thought is was exciting at the time, forgetting how terrible it could have been for my brothers.

As I write my story, I think about how we have destroyed so many natural resources like our ponds and rivers, as during our trip to the tip we were able to break a piece of straw and suck water from ditches without fear of the water being polluted.

We finally arrived at the tip and fortunately it was quite deserted, so we set about our search for jam jars and cycle parts. Brian spent his time taking old bikes apart while Ken and I climbed through the rubbish collecting the jars. The smell was disgusting as there was every kind of thing there, including newly dumped horse heads. By the time we collected all we wanted and we had washed the jars it was late afternoon. We made our way back home and hid the jars in Ken's father's shed: we had a great day and made plenty of pennies.

'Where have you been all day?' shouted Ken's mum, standing at the back door. 'Hurry up and wash your hands, your tea is ready.'

With that I made my way to the back gate to go home not realising I was included.

'Come on Keith, you too,' she cried.

I was so pleased as I had forgotten how hungry I was. We had egg and chips and it was lovely. After tea a bath was prepared and again I shared in turn with the boys. Brian was about the same build as myself, so his mum again gave me two shirts and a pair of trousers for the return to school. She even trimmed and washed my hair again.

I never wanted to go home, but it was now early evening and I thought I had better go as I had been out since early morning, and could already be in trouble. As I was leaving, Ken's mum put her arms around me, telling me to take care and thanked me for looking after Brian. Although so young, it felt lovely and I realised that this sort of closeness was missing in my life. To this day I believe just to hold the hand of someone you love is so wonderful, one can have a relationship for life and not know what love is and that is so sad.

I made my way down the street for home, carrying a brown bag containing my new shirts and trousers: I decided to go the back way so that I could hide my clothes in one of the garden sheds to avoid my dad seeing them. Fortunately, my dad had gone out for a beer so I managed to bring my new clothes in to show my mum. She was pleased but I think she felt a bit awkward. She noticed my haircut and how clean I looked but never commented as my brothers were there, and she knew they would say something when my dad came home. It was a bit late but I sat down and ate my Sunday dinner, which my mum warmed up for me, not telling her I had already been fed. I still wanted to ask my mum about yesterday and how she felt, but it was a bit difficult with my brothers being there.

Tomorrow would be the last day of our school holidays, and then a change of classes for us all. It had been a wonderful summer and for my friends, and me and a very profitable one in our modest way.

I met Brian and Ken early the next morning ready to deliver our jam jars to Moody's. We had again done well and were very pleased with our little scheme. In future it would be purely a Sunday adventure, apart from holidays. As for myself, I would be starting my milk round job the next Saturday.

Because we were back to school tomorrow, we thought we would treat ourselves to a bag of fish and chips, which we ate while sitting on the church wall in Filton. We felt quite chuffed having money in our pockets.

It was now early afternoon and we made our way home to prepare for school the next day. My mum met me at the door, telling me my bath was ready and would I like to use it first before my brothers shared it. What bath I thought as it was full of coal. To my surprise the coal had been emptied and cleaned that morning by my mum. I think she had a real hard life trying so hard to keep us all together in those difficult days.

It was a long time since my mum washed my back but it was good, apart from being bathed with Fairy washing soap, and Derbac soap for my hair. It took my thoughts back to the Convent and the big lady in her rubber apron. Later that day was a day of great revelation to me, as I was to overhear shocking details about our families plight and the reasons for our many unexplained situations.

It was now mid afternoon, and the three of us had our baths.

'Don't get dirty,' my mum shouted as I escaped out to the back garden.

I still had about eight shillings in my pocket so decided to crawl into my hideaway and retrieve my tobacco tin. I kept sixpence for the next day and hid the rest.

In the garden we had two sheds and a chicken run containing four hens and a cockerel named Henry. He was so friendly, at times, and I was able to sit next to him on the straw out of sight from anyone. As I sat there feeling all cosy and clean my brothers came out into the garden and sat nearby on my dad's homemade bench seat.

'Where's he gone?' meaning me of course.

I kept quiet and said nothing as they sat there for quite sometime. Eventually my brother Ron asked Bill where my dad was.

'With the twins of course.'

What are they talking about I thought, what twins? Being reluctant to give my hiding place away I kept still until we were called in for tea following them in five minutes later.

When we went to bed I told them I was in next door's garden earlier with my friend Alan when I heard them talking about twins and asked them to tell me what it was all about. Even though I must have been quite a tearaway, I was quite sensitive about telling lies and always felt guilty. However, they were reluctant to tell me and started thumping and bullying me and told me I was too young to know. As I have said before, Ron was very handy with his fists and that night continued to punch me in the arm until I fell on the floor in tears, for the first time Bill stepped in and stopped it and said I had a right to know about my twin brothers.

With that my mum came into the bedroom wondering what the noise was about. Although still in tears, I pretended to be asleep and waited for her to go, eventually, Bill came over and explained as much as he knew. First, he made me promise never to tell anyone else what he was about to say and to this day as I write my story, this is the first time I have done so. Apparently, in those days, illegitimacy was frowned upon far, far more then than it is today.

I was to learn that my father had a relationship with a lady friend at the BAC a number of years before, which led to her pregnancy and the birth of twin boys. To this day I have never met them and don't even know if they are still alive. Being only ten years old I never quite understood the real potential of this problem, and its implications. All of this had been the beginning of the family breakdown and the loss of our home in the earlier years. For whatever reason my father was not always in a financial position to maintain the twins and for this had ended up in prison. This explained the reason for so many traumas that affected us all in the past and in the future.

While Bill was explaining the situation, I told him about my visit to my gran's and what happened, and asked if he knew why mum and my aunt avoided each other.

'You must promise again if I tell you, not to say anything,' said Bill, and I agreed.

He explained that my father was courting my aunt for a while, and then my mum came along and became his new girlfriend. This created a love triangle many details of which we will never know. I don't wish to know as I believe that love is a private affair that can be wonderful but can also be so cruel.

I lay there in bed for ages thinking about everything and was wondering if other families had these sort of problems. My mum always said, you will never know what goes on behind closed doors, and I guess that's so true; it was certainly true of my family.

I awoke very early the next morning, before anyone else, and I got dressed for school. I had to wait for my porridge as all the food was locked away as usual. My mum came down first followed by dad, in a hurry.

'Don't get in his way, he's late for work,' mum whispered, and with that I quickly disappeared through the back door to the garden.

I felt so hungry waiting for my breakfast that I pulled a couple of carrots, which I could do without getting in trouble as I had grown them in the first place. Even with some dirt on them, they still tasted lovely. I eventually had my porridge and left for school carrying my brown paper bag containing jam sandwiches, without butter or margarine. I hated them, as by lunchtime the jam would soak into the bread, however some days it never mattered as I was too hungry to care. I don't recall seeing plastic bags in those days, so quite often, the jam would also soak through the brown bag and the sandwiches would end up on the pavement. I always picked them up though, regardless.

School meals were six pence a day each for me, my brothers and my sister, so this was beyond our reach. Fortunately, because of my jam jar income I would treat myself at least three times a week to a meal except on a Friday as they served sago, which I hated, even if I was hungry. Some days, Ken and I would get on the bus to Filton Park to buy a loaf to fill with chips.

So far in my story I have made very little reference to my two sisters living at home. They too found life very difficult at times sharing the same traumas like hunger and uncertainty. If I recall correctly my older sister Hilda was already at work. Barbara, the younger sister, was still at school with us. She too has stories relating to hunger. One day she was so hungry she stole an apple from the same shop that I took my jam jars to, and ran all the way home, throwing the apple away for fear of being caught and going to prison. The fear of strict retaliation from police and parents was a deterrent at that time, but as children we were still dishonest by telling an occasional lie or two.

One day, my mum sent Barbara shopping to buy some potatoes and gave her two shillings. On the way, Barbara lost the money and was too scared to go home. Eventually she decided to make up a story saying she was robbed by a boy. Mum believed her and decided to call the police, not quite sure what happened, but Barbara dug herself out of a hole somehow even though the loss was genuine, that's the fear we all had.

My first day back at school was a very mixed one as I had to move to the senior class and it took all day before we were settled in. I was to sit next to a girl called Kitty, and we were to stay great friends throughout the rest of my time at school. She was quite an attractive girl and most of the boys in class took a shine to her. I remember being punched in the nose one day just for spending time with her in the playground.

The first week back to school was fine but the second week was horrendous as the school nurse turned up and sent some of us home because of nits in our hair. I cried all the way home fearing what my dad would do. My mum immediately boiled some water and gave my hair a good scrub. I was dreading my dad coming home as he was due in and, as I feared, he dragged me into the back garden and cut most of my hair off.

'Please don't hit him Bill,' mum shouted.

'Now wash his hair again,' said dad in anger. 'After that you can go to bed you dirty little sod with no tea.'

I was trembling and did as he told me. I had to stay away from school for a whole week before I could see the nurse again to get the all clear.

I eventually saw her and she was pleased with the effort made and said I could come back to school in another week's time.

These days we know how horrible children can be to each other, but I feel it was just as serious then as I was to go through some very cruel situations upon my return to school. It started in the playground on the first day back when they started calling me 'Ragamuffin' and 'Baldy'. Some might say I should have punched them in the nose, but that was not my way as I saw enough of that in my own home with my father and brothers. I have snapped once, but that was much later on in my life while in the RAF, facing five bullies all at the same time.

Kitty was always nice to me and said not to worry as her brother was sent home for the same thing. Apparently they were quite well off and lived in a big house and were able to have a bath every day.

Without poking a finger directly at anyone, I tried to explain what was going on to my teacher but was told not to tell tales and I was threatened with the cane. I stood it for the rest of the week but the following Monday I played truant which I continued for about three weeks: the longer I did it the more scared I became of a visit from the school inspector and my parents finding out.

Every morning I would go out as normal and hide under a gun turret, which was still operational at the time. It was located near the tip where we collected our jam jars. Some days I would collect a few and hide them for the Sunday. Some days I would raid my money tin and get the bus for Old Market and visit the News Theatre to watch The Lone Ranger and The Scarlet Horseman. At that time my father left the BAC and went back to his trade as bricklayer. This was fatal for me as one morning I was walking down the mile stretch as we called it and nearly walked right into him and his work colleague. I made a dash for the hedge thinking he had not seen me. I was wrong.

'Keith,' he called. 'See you tonight at home.'

With that I ran all the way home and told my mum what I had been doing and why. Perhaps I really was bad in those days, I just don't know what to think, and maybe I got what I deserved - who knows?

As always, my mum was more understanding, but she was a bit worried about a dreaded visit from the school inspector and was quite cross with me, I found it difficult to lie to her so told her it was three weeks since I went to school. To my father I lied, and told him that I was late and afraid to go to school that morning. I think my father must have had other things on his mind that day, as what I had done seemed of little importance to him.

I considered myself lucky on that occasion, so I decided to face the abuse at school regardless. I returned to school the next day with three weeks hair growth, and it appeared that the novelty had worn off apart from the normal bullies having an occasional dig. We did have a home visit from the school inspector, but my dad was not at home. It was again fortunate for me and with that in mind I kept my head down for the rest of the term.

Summer was coming to an end. Ken, Brian and I continued our little schemes, including my Saturday morning job with the milkman. Every other Saturday I would visit my gran in St. Paul's Bristol, but without mum. In view of what I had learnt during the last month, I never asked again about my mum's secret or about the twins. I very often wonder what my unknown brothers did in their life, but this I shall never know, even if they are still alive.

Death comes to us all one day but some people can't accept that fact and avoid talking about it, thinking it will go away. My gran died suddenly and I wasn't told for another week until I was about to catch a bus to see her. All week I was being told to give it a miss this week - why?

Following on from the shock of being told, Brian had one of his fits while we were at the tip one Sunday, and was ill for a while. Sadly, he was to end up in a special hospital for many years to come, and in another part of the country, and I never saw him again. He was always making us laugh, and we missed him very much.

With winter on its way, we concentrated on building up all the bicycle parts we had left, as our garden sheds were getting untidy. It was only a matter of time before we were told off about that. We used what we could and put the rest out for the rubbish man. If they only knew where it came from we thought!

We finally assembled four bikes. One of them I had to deliver to Eastville, where we were to be paid £4.10 shillings. I don't know if you have ever cycled along and pulled another bike alongside, but I can assure you it's not easy. While I was riding down Muller Road I picked up speed and the bike I was pulling on my left started bouncing causing me to sway from side to side. As I got closer to the bus station I was so scared I just let it go, and it reared down straight into the side of a bus. Worrying about the damage it might have done, I peddled like mad down Muller Road, turning left for Lockleze and back to Filton. I wonder what happened to that bike?

5

Revenge

Revenge was never my way but sometimes the hurt was so much, and uncalled for, that I would get very angry and say or do things that I was so sorry for later, even to this day. Perhaps it's the hatred I have for bullies. I don't know.

One Saturday evening my father came home late after drinking and set about my brothers and me for no reason. I was still sobbing the next morning as I left very early to go to Ken's house. We were due to go to the tip but decided not to. I sat talking to Ken's mum for a while, where I had one of those rare cuddles. She said I could stay to dinner, which I know would have been lovely, but thought I had better go home. I walked down the street towards home but stopped on the corner wondering what to do. I sat on the wall with all sorts of thoughts going through my mind, mainly, would I be in trouble if I went home. With thoughts of revenge in my head I thought that I could no longer take anymore beatings and I walked two miles to the nearest Police Station. At first they treated me like someone unable to take a normal household smack, but I explained in more detail what had been going on.

After an hour or so a police car took me home, dropping me a street away so that my father would be unaware. They explained that if he started on me when I got home I should run out of the house as they were not allowed to enter a home but could arrest him outside if he followed me.

I entered my front door feeling assured they were going to wait around for an hour. I never felt proud of what I did but enough was enough. My mum was pleased to see me and wondered where I had been, my dad was asleep in the armchair so all was quiet for at least the afternoon.

The police told me to keep my head down and not give him any excuse to pick on me. For a while I disappeared out into my hideaway in the garden and did just that. My mum eventually called me in for tea where I sat very quiet eating dripping sandwiches. The peace and quiet didn't last as my father angrily asked me if I was sulking.

'No!' I shouted in anger.

With that he told me not to answer back then stood up, and I knew what was about to happen next.

'You did ask me a question Dad,' I cried.

With that I made for the front door with him following me. He caught me on the front path but stumbled spilling all his loose change on the lawn and border. I ran so fast up the street I felt that my heart was in my mouth and feared that I could never go home again. With this in mind, I reached the phone box and rang the police. It took me ages to explain the situation as I was shaking all over. The police remembered me and arrived at the phone box within ten minutes.

By then I was wondering if I had gone too far and wished I had not gone through with it, however the police took me home and enticed my dad out of the house for a long chat. They sat him in the police car for ages releasing him about an hour later. As he came in I stood behind my mum fearing he would have his revenge on me. To my surprise he never said a word. I was so relieved. I was not proud of what I did and even to this day I have regrets about it, but at the time I was unable to cope with any more beatings.

During the night I heard my dad having a row with my mum. I guess it was about me and what I had done. My brothers were very shocked about what I did and said they would blame me if he got worse.

The next morning I was to do my father a further injustice. As I was leaving for school and closing the front door I noticed something glittering on the side border of the lawn. To my surprise, I found not one, but two half crowns lying on their edges,. Straight away I remembered my dad dropping his money, so I guess the money must have belonged to him.

Although feeling very guilty, yet still feeling angry with my dad, I decided to keep it for revenge. Believe it or not, even to this very day I think of my dad regarding this injustice, and wished I could have told him what I did but could never get close enough to do so for fear of reprisal.

The only consolation I have was the fact that he took six shillings and eight pence off me later in the future, claiming that I had too much money for a boy my age. This was my weeks wages from a paper job I was to take on. Perhaps in my father's mind, his treatment of me, was discipline, but to me it was bullying, especially with the extremes he went to.

The incredible outcome of this latest incident was the fact that my father never touched me again, and we were to become closer in many ways. With the new relationship we shared, I was to help him with his building jobs that he took on to earn extra money. Many of the jobs were brick laying and concrete paths. I learnt quite a lot, much of which I still remember to this day. I would spend many hours after school collecting hardcore for foundations and various other jobs, in preparation for when he arrived home. I really loved it, as well as earning a few extra shillings.

Ken and I still carried on with our little money-making schemes, and I even found time to keep the back garden tidy for my mum.

6

War is Over

Although the war was at an end, life continued to be a struggle at home. My brothers, sisters and I were even scoffed at when we went to the street party empty handed, expecting to share with the rest of the street children. Even though my dad was in regular employment now I think it was a case of trying to catch up financially, but never getting there.

Most people were forced to buy clothes and essentials through what we called a tallyman. They paid him six pence a week to clear the debt, which in some cases went on for years: the clothes were often worn out before they were paid for. When I think back, we even lacked simple things such as cups as most of the time we drank out of jam jars, I ask myself - how did we get there? I guess that when you're down, you're down.

Being so young, we could only think about our lot, and forgot that most families were struggling too. Communication in that era was very limited and we had no idea what was going on in the rest of the world. We all know now, and it makes our war lives a tea party in comparison.

A number of years passed, bringing me to the age of fourteen. Nothing had changed at home and life continued in much the same way. My brothers had already started work, bringing some much needed money home to my mum. Ken and I still carried on with our schemes, but spent less time at the tip. For some time now we both had an after school paper selling job outside the BAC at Filton, for which I was paid six shillings and eight pence a week.

My relationship with dad continued in the right direction, but for my brothers there was often friction: they had come of age and were in a position of being able to retaliate violently if provoked.

Sadly, my dad was again arrested for violence, and unknown to him, I was to witness the whole incident.

My friend Kitty, who I palled up with when I started in the senior school, was still my closest friend. Now and again we would go to the pictures on a Saturday night and share fish and chips as we walked home, and I can still taste them now. As we were walking towards Filton shopping area one Saturday night, I saw a tall man in a black overcoat walking about fifty yards in front. Suddenly I realised it was my dad. Out of nowhere arrived a police car and two policemen jumped out. One was a constable, the other an inspector. The police grabbed my dad from behind as he passed Mill's grocery shop, but not knowing who they were, he immediately turned and punched one officer straight through the glass door of the shop - followed shortly by the other. My dad calmly walked home as though nothing had happened. By the time the police arrived to arrest him at about midnight we were all in bed. We feared the worst. Not meaning to sound selfish, I always thought that all of this was only happening to me, but what must my poor mum have made of all this, bless her.

I was later to learn that my dad was sitting on his own in the saloon bar at the Anchor pub, which was his regular. It seems the bar was full and every table covered with glasses of beer. Apparently he was accused of drinking out of a glass belonging to someone else. He claimed that this was not the case and if it bothered them that much, he would buy them a fresh one. The person refused and continued to torment and embarrass him in front of several people. As I see it, being in the shoes of the tormentor, I would have thought twice about my actions as my father was built like a brick toilet, to put it politely.

My dad left the pub about 10.30 pm and waited outside for his accuser. He finally came out and my dad approached him, asking for an apology, but the guy just laughed in my dad's face, so he beat him up and 'knocked him straight into next week' as the phrase goes. The police released my dad during the night, but to this day I never knew about the outcome of his actions.

7

Hope and Fear

Now at the age of fourteen, life at home seemed to take on new meaning as my outlook and thoughts were now more mature, although for sometime I had a feeling of hopelessness, and I feared the future.

My mum continued to be my closest friend always finding time to have a chat with me. One day when in one of her emotional moments she told me how I nearly died at birth, and that after a week she was told to go home as there was very little hope for me. Apparently, she refused and nursed me through: on the funnier side, she said I did look like a scrawny rabbit.

After my father had been arrested there was a period of calm in the household, and it was only a matter of time before he would again return to his old self. Everyone was treading on eggshells but it finally happened, and it started with me. It was a Friday evening when I arrived home after completing my paper job. Showing my mum my wages of 6s 8d, my father suddenly turned on me saying that I had too much money for a boy my age and that I was getting too big for my boots. He took the money from me which I never saw again. Fortunately, I had money in my tin so was still able to meet Kitty and go to the cinema as we had planned. In those days I recall that beer was 10d a pint and rough cider was 8d, so I guess my 6s 8d bought my dad quite a few ciders. The next day, Saturday, my father finished work at noon as usual and went straight to the pub not returning home until late at night. That weekend must have been the worst of our lives. None of us had any idea what was about to happen.

As I approached my house that evening I passed my sister Hilda kissing her boyfriend goodnight on the corner. Hoping all was quiet at home I went through the door to find my brothers were already there. Even though we were much older now my mum asked us to go to bed just to keep the peace in case of any trouble.

I don't quite remember if my sister came in on time, but my brothers and I lay awake in our beds chatting away when my father fell through the door. He was quiet for a while but the peace didn't last long as he called the three of us downstairs, asking us why we had disappeared upstairs. My mum tried to protect us by standing between him and us but he lashed out regardless knocking her in the face. This was his last big mistake as the two sons he taught to fight turned on him and gave him a beating he would never forget. He was finally knocked out by falling on to the tiled fireplace. I ask myself to this day, if this was when I developed my hatred for bullies. The same night both Bill and Ron left home never to return again. From the domestic point of view, they both had jobs bringing home much needed money for my mum and this was now all gone besides all the hurt.

Apart from the bit of love my mum could show me I was sadly missing something in my life but never knew what. I always think and wish to this day that we could be at peace with everyone. I used to fantasise when I was younger to the extent that if I was in charge of the United Nations there would be no wars. What a wonderful dream. After that terrible night I don't ever recall my father being violent again, in fact I think it broke him forever despite everything. I love my dad and hope there is such a thing as an after life when I can tell him so.

For a while, life at home reached some normality, apart from a shortage of money. I occasionally went to a jumble sale with my mum to fit myself out for school, but even that was becoming difficult as most people were doing the same thing. Ken and I were still making some money, so I was able to buy my own bits and pieces; in fact I could get a pair of trousers for just three pence.

I used to be able to talk to Mr. Robinson, the milkman, about anything, especially my home problems. One Saturday morning he asked me if I would like go along to a new chapel he was opening on Filton Hill the following Sunday. There would be a lot of young people my age and he thought I would enjoy it. He never mentioned it before and I had no idea that he was a Christian, but his idea was to lead me to a new way of life away from the constant torment and upset at home.

The chapel was quite tiny, and for the first Sunday the twelve other children and I spent all our time cleaning and preparing for the following weekend. The stone walls were dusty with cobwebs which could have been a hundred years old at least. It smelt quite damp, but the beauty of it was so wonderful when the sun's rays shone through the tiny windows, half covered with dead moths and such like. Outside the chapel the grass and tall wild flowers were partly covering old gravestones with their old inscriptions barely readable. I felt so at peace there and would forget what normally troubled me until I went home. For the first time for so long I really felt a part of something important.

When we had finished the cleaning it occurred to some of us that their was no organ or a piano. Mr. Robinson explained that we had neither and would have to improvise. At that time I had never heard of the word improvise, and thought I would wait and see. He was quite a clever man as we were to see at our first chapel service.

I could hardly wait for the next Sunday to arrive; it was all I could think of during the week. On the Saturday, while delivering milk, I tried to find out more but was told it would be a surprise. The Sunday school was to start at 3pm but I was the very first there at just after two. I sat on a gravestone for a while in the glorious sunshine feeling so happy. After a short while I decided to explore the stone cottages behind the churchyard, which matched the church stonework. I guess it was quite a community many years before and I tried to imagine what must have been like.

At the side of the graveyard was a rough stony path and I decided to venture even further down to a narrow archway that lead into a large open space, well cultivated with flower and vegetable gardens. There was not a soul in sight for a while as I sat on a stonewall feeling the hot sun on my back. Then I heard a lady's voice asking me what I was doing. I panicked and said I needed a drink of water, asking if she knew the time as I might be late for church. I think she was pleased to hear the church part, and was very nice to me. She told me the time and brought me out an empty glass which was a bit confusing, but she smiled and said I would have to use the garden pump which took my thoughts back to Tockington when I was five years old. I felt so happy that it seemed as if I had been there for hours, but it was only twenty minutes. When I said goodbye the lady said I could call again if I wanted to, which I did so many times after that, which lead to a great friendship with her grandson.

Feeling refreshed, I made my way back up the stony footpath to the chapel where I was still the first to have arrived. Five minutes later Mr. Robinson turned up carrying some sort of holdall. He withdrew a very large key to unlock the chapel door. The door creaked as he pushed it open, showing its age.

As we entered I could feel the heat of the sun coming through the tiny windows. I guessed they had not been opened for many years, that's if they would open at all. It was so quiet for a short while until the other children started turning up. There were about thirty of us all together including some parents, some had brought flowers to brighten the place up a bit.

I remember the very first hymn being Yes, Jesus Loves Me, but we all looked at each other wondering where the music would come from. Suddenly, Mr. Robinson retrieved a saw and a violin bow from his carpenter's bag and started to play it by bending the saw and running the bow over it as one would with a violin. It sounded great and completely in tune, we were all astounded as we all began to sing.

It was a super afternoon and I think everyone loved it, including all the parents. Being a bit sensitive about my clothes I did notice that many of the children were much better dressed than I was, which made me feel a bit inadequate. The following Saturday I went to a jumble sale where I bought my first pair of long trousers for half a crown and they fitted me perfectly, although Ken's mum had offered to alter them for me.

When my sister Hilda saw them she said how nice they looked and that I could do with a sports jacket to match now that I was going to Chapel. She showed me a jacket that was too small for her and she asked if I would like it. I can picture it now, being a dark green with a tiny check pattern. To me it was lovely and I wore it the very next Sunday. Being a bit ignorant of fashion, I was not aware that ladies buttoned jackets on the other side, until a less friendly person made a meal of it in front of some of my friends. I coped with it however, and wore it for quite sometime. The jacket seemed to trigger off further changes in my life as without it, would I have been noticed?

I attended the chapel for several months without a miss, and loved it so much. I was always first there and the last to leave. One day Mr. Robinson said that he attended a Baptist Chapel on a Sunday evening as well, and would I like to go too. It was located in Filton Avenue and run by a Dr. Packer, who was to help me so much in my life in the months to come. For all this I thank Mr. Robinson.

8

The Coat of Many Colours

After my first visit to the Baptist chapel I asked Mr. Robinson if he minded if I went to Filton one Sunday, and to Filton Avenue the following week. He said it would be fine, but that I would be missed. The following week I arrived early at the Baptist church ready for the afternoon Sunday school. Most of the young people were much older than me and I noticed again how nicely dressed they were too.

After the service I mixed in with everyone, but I was aware of some of the girls looking at me. I could guess what they were talking about. I stood there for a while, speechless and nearly in tears. Suddenly, to my relief, I heard a loud voice behind me.

'Ah, this must be Keith.' It was Dr. Packer and his wife introducing themselves.

'I saw you in the main chapel last week with Mr. Robinson,' said Dr. Packer. 'I just hope you will feel at home here.'

His wife gave me a big smile, but I am sure she too was looking at my jacket as I undid the buttons not to give the game away, but she was no fool. Perhaps I became paranoid with the nature of my coat now I was in more refined surroundings, but unfortunately, I had very little else to wear.

As I was leaving through the chapel gate Mrs. Packer called me back and asked me if I would like to go to tea at their house the following Saturday. I had never been to a large, smart house before, but I agreed and said I would love to. The week seemed to last a lifetime but Saturday arrived at last. I cycled there on one of my better bikes and arrived on time. It was nice to sit at a table and have a proper meal with a tablecloth and nice cutlery.

After tea we talked for quite a while but I was still aware of Mrs. Packer looking at me, still wearing my 'coat of many colours' as I decided to call it. I think her motive was a kind one when she started to ask and enquire about my clothing sizes, but I didn't have a clue as I had never had any new clothes bought from a shop in my life before. After a lovely afternoon, I left and cycled home where my mum was waiting to hear all about it. I had to pick my words carefully as like most mums, they can feel left out if one was to say how happy and well fed they were in another person's household, especially back in that era.

Monday was soon upon us and I was back to school. I never took the chance and didn't wear my coat as I knew what I would have been in for if I had: most kids were alright but there was always a few spoilers.

Ken and I met at the school gate as we did each weekday afternoon before going off to sell our newspapers at the BAC Filton. We were still doing our jar collection too, mainly when we were running a bit short of pocket money. When I arrived home on Tuesday from my paper job my mum opened the front door before I got halfway down the path. She had a smile on her face in some sort of anticipation of something special about to happen.

'Look,' she cried. 'It's for you.'

On the table was a huge brown paper parcel.

'What's in it?' I cried with excitement.

'Clothes, from Doctor Packer. You just missed him,' my mum explained.

All of a sudden I was aware of someone in the kitchen and realised it was my brother Ron visiting while my dad was at work. He had a tormenting grin on his face as he pushed me aside, making for the front door. He looked a bit guilty as he left, and I was to discover the reason for this a little later. I excitedly returned to my parcel discovering that it had already been opened. I cut the rest of the string and to my amazement it was full of clothes, some of them hardly worn. I was so excited about the clothes, it never really occurred to me why the parcel was partly opened until my mother felt that she had to tell me what had happened. Apparently my brother had opened it and helped himself to some of the items: I would have shared the parcel with him if he had asked, but sadly nothing had changed.

In a selfish way I was not sorry that my brothers had left home as I finally had a bed and a whole bedroom to myself. I did miss Bill a little, as we had got on okay when he and I were together, but for the first time in the house I was able to get to know my sisters Hilda and Barbara a bit better. The household for a while became much quieter, but the future was to hold yet another sting in the tail to devastate us all.

Now that my two brothers were no longer bringing wages home to my mum, money again became short and after a while my mum said she could no longer give me six pence a day for my dinner at school. I was quite happy to pay for myself, but she would not hear of it, and said that I had to come home each lunchtime for my meal.

This I did for a while but through my own fault I clashed with the Headmaster for being late back to school two afternoons on the trot. On my travels back to class I, and most other children, used to play on a haystack near the school, and this was well known by the teachers. As I entered my class ten minutes late on the second occasion my teacher cried.

'Don't sit down, you horrible child. Go straight to the headmasters office, he is waiting for you.'

'But Miss I cried,' nearly wetting myself.

'Don't answer back,' she shouted, as she pushed me out of the classroom door poking me in the back with her lead pencil which went through my thin shirt into my back and into my flesh; it was sore for days.

Already in tears with the stinging of the pencil jab I climbed the dreaded staircase to the headmaster's office. I was met by his assistant who was really nice, as she could see I was already stressed out and knowing the headmasters reputation for caning.

I don't know if there were any laws on caning procedures in those days but he was well known for swinging the cane back as far as possible over his shoulder before plunging it onto a person's hand. I was not sure to this day if he was going to cane me, and I might have brought it upon myself as he asked me if I had been on the haystack that day, and already in pain I said no. With this he warned me that if I moved my hand I would get two strokes.

'Stretch your hand out straight,' he shouted in anger as he raised his cane right over his back to his waistline, finally lunging it into my open palm.

'That's for telling lies as well because you have straw sticking out of your shoe.'

I never knew what passing out meant but at that moment I nearly did as the pain was more than I could bear as I made my sorry way back to my class. I carefully knocked on my classroom door waiting for permission to enter, as we had to in those days. The teacher was very manly and wore bloomers, as the boys would observe. She came to the door and saw that I was in no fit state to continue class that afternoon, apart from anything else I wouldn't be able to hold a pen or pencil. She suggested I sat in the corridor for the rest of the day. As I turned away in the direction of a much needed chair she asked me what I had on my shirt at the back and had I fallen off the haystack.

'It's covered in blood,' she said, but I never answered her question because I was scared that I might get the cane again if I said she did it.

'I think you had better go home as its still bleeding, and partly stuck to your back,' she said. 'Do you want the caretaker to take you home in his car?'

I was so angry I wanted to say something nasty or tell her where to go but again in those days it was more than you would ever dare to.

'No thank you Miss, I will make my way home on my own.'

I made my way out of school, up the road and across the cornfield, which was the shortest way home for me, I don't think I went near that haystack again during my school days over the rest of that summer. Although I wasn't physically crying, the pain in my hand made me sob for the rest of the day, I was just hoping that my mum would not be there when I got home as I know I would have broken down if she had come near me.

Fortunately there was no one home when I arrived and I managed to climb through the toilet window so that I could wash and change my shirt. I managed to pull my shirt off but it was blood stained over a large area, I just stood there in my trousers for ages wondering what to do. Suddenly, I thought of the clothes parcel that Doctor Packer brought me and knew there were shirts that I could change into without anyone knowing.

We had no ready hot water in the house to wash my shirt so I tried to wash it in cold but the stain got even worse. Eventually I decided to bury it deep in my garden so that no one would be any the wiser.

An hour had passed and I was still on my own so decided to slip out the back way, then up the road to my paper job at the BAC Filton. It was difficult to let my friend Ken know what had happened but he turned up eventually, even though a bit late. I only had to sell eight dozen papers but it felt like a hundred dozen, my hand was so sore and made it so difficult to even pick up one paper.

I think that day was the most dreadful school day of my life, as although not always being the best behaved pupil, I had never had the cane before and never wanted it again. When I arrived home it was not long before my mum guessed there was something wrong, eventually bringing me to tears. When my father came in he asked her what was wrong with me.

'Serve him bloody right,' he shouted.

With that response I thought, nothing has really changed has it.

Wartime newspaper placards

A typical Bristol shop window 1941, taped to reduce flying glass

City centre bomb damage

Anderson Shelter, named after Sir John Anderson Home Secretary

Metal for munitions collection

Time for a game of cricket

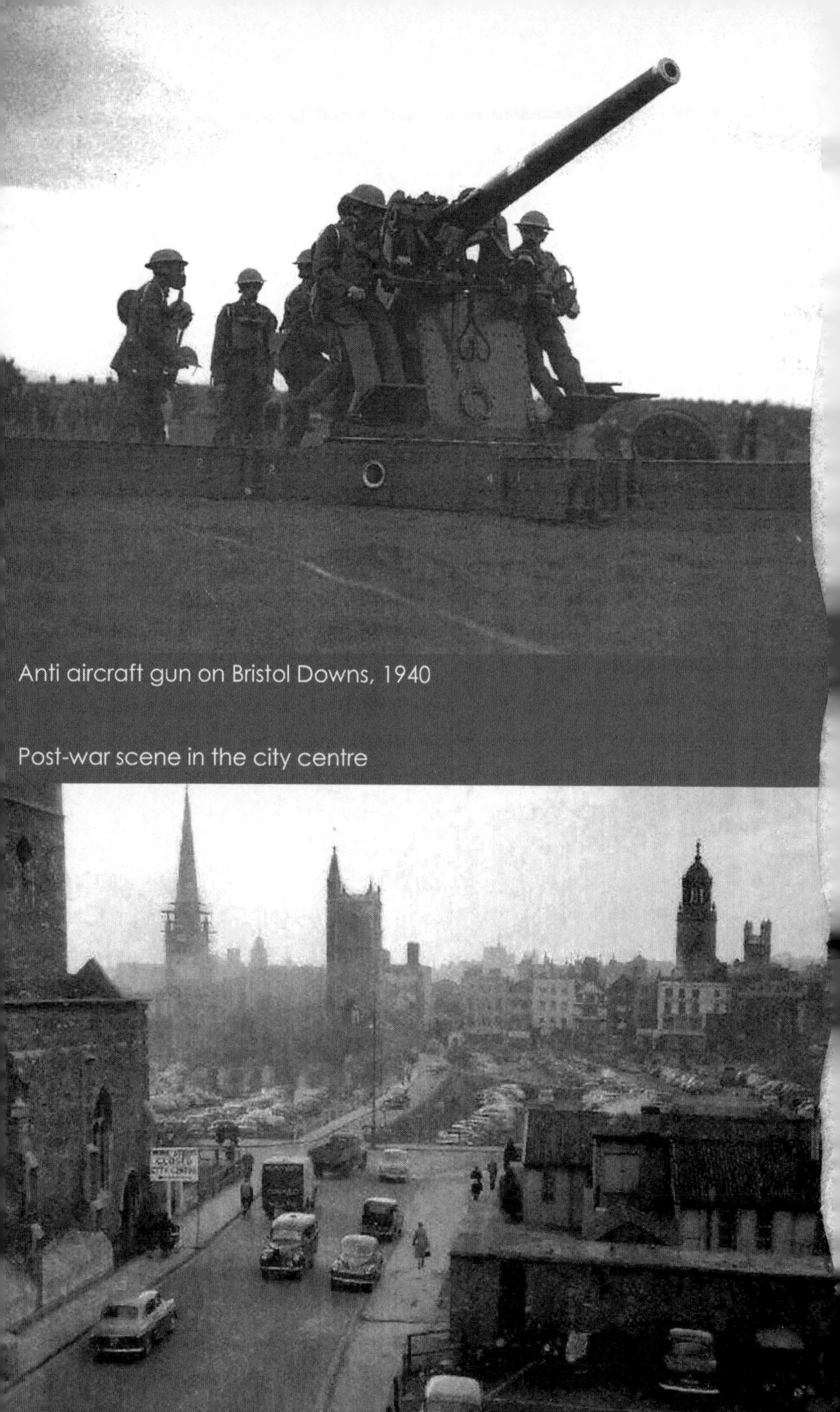

Anti aircraft gun on Bristol Downs, 1940

Post-war scene in the city centre

9

Turning the Corner

With the introduction of my new friends, Mr. Robinson, Doctor Packer and his wife, my whole attitude to life and the way I lived it gradually changed in many ways. I started to feel that life was so much better than it used to be. Because of the clothes I was given I felt quite proud of myself and became a fanatic about personal hygiene: years before I would not wash for days if I could help it.

When I went to chapel on Sunday evenings, I was so proud to stand up and do a reading from the Bible in front of anyone, including the girls who used to chatter about my coat of many colours. It was difficult to believe that I was the same person as that little pathetic lad in the convent being washed and deloused, which seemed to be a lifetime ago.

As the weeks passed I became more confident in many ways. If people were unkind to me I would normally retaliate verbally, but this mattered no more. I just can't describe the feeling. I even started trying to understand my father's and brothers' aggression, but found that difficult as both of my brothers had improved their boxing skills and started to fight in competitions. They were very good, but I think Ron was more a fighter than a boxer. I was to see them in action in an American fair that used to be located in a nearby field at the end of our street for two weeks every year. They brought with them twelve boxers who would take on all-comers over those two weeks. Ron knocked out eight of them, Bill was not so fortunate.

Within a year, Ron became the bantamweight champion of the west of England. He lived for boxing for many years, but ill health was to take its toll on him after suffering various injuries related to constant beatings to the body; this however, he would never admit. Over the next few months and years I was to see very little of my brothers as each went their own way. Sadly, apart from my sister Barbara, my family to this day only contact each other if someone is dying or has died.

With the absence of my brothers and their income, there were signs of financial desperation. One day I arrived home from school to see my mother cutting into a polish tin lid and crafting it into the size of a shilling, which she could put into the gas or electric meter. This was quite a common practice in those days as there were always rebates when the boxes were emptied providing it was not taken up by too many homemade tokens. Unfortunately some people had put too many in and were unable to pay the difference, leading to their supply being turned off.

With my life changing for the better, it was difficult knowing that at times I had more money in my tobacco tin than my mum had in her purse. I offered to pay for things, but she would not hear of it. Sometimes however, we would go to the Cabot Cinema together and I would pay for her, and buy fish and chips for us afterwards. I was always so proud as we walked home arm in arm on a Friday evening.

In the middle of all this sadness there were some funny moments, as I was to discover one day to my embarrassment. One evening, after arriving home from my paper job, Doctor Packer had delivered another big parcel containing more clothes. Fortunately my brother Ron was not there, so the package had remained intact. To my excitement, it contained a very expensive brown Harris Tweed jacket and overcoat, with velvet collars. I was so excited, until I tried it on. My father let out this loud laugh, pointing out that both coats had hump backs. Even my mum had to smile but not unkindly. I looked in the old fashioned mirror hanging above the fireplace and saw the funny side of it. There could have been a sad story of the person who they came from, but I never found that out. I had the coats altered eventually, but was never allowed to forget the story to this very day.

Today is Sunday and Ken and I make our final trip to the tip for our jam jars. The shopkeeper had told us that he would not be taking them much longer as during the war there was a need for them, but the demand was now decreasing. We had done very well over the years and would never complain. It seemed very strange to be at the tip for the last time, despite the horrible smells, the horse heads and the flies. I was dressed a little better now, which made me reluctant to climb onto the tip. The end of the tip visits worked out quite well for both of us. We were close to the age of leaving school and were already having job interviews. Ken was going to be an apprentice at the BAC and I was going into the building trade as a plumber's mate.

The last two months at school were good. Winding down was almost a pleasure as we were allowed quite a bit of free time to do whatever we enjoyed doing. I enjoyed athletics quite a lot but was politely reminded that I was spending too much time with the girls, and if I liked them that much I could join them in the weekly knitting lessons. The thought of that delighted me, but after six weeks the only pattern I had learnt to knit was plain - I can't imagine why.

I could have stayed on at school if I had wanted to, but in those times an extra wage earner in the house was far more important. As dad reminded me, it was time I started to bring some money home for my mother.

My family were not very communicative regarding what was going on in the household. I felt that there were things still hidden from me, just like they had always been in the past, although I had no idea what was lurking in the background. I asked myself why it had to be like that. I was so glad I had my friends at the chapel to turn to on a Sunday.

. . . .

On the day I was to meet my new employer, at his house in Filton Avenue, I dressed up smartly and even had a haircut at a hairdressers for the first time, which cost six pence.

'I'm Mr. Tom Parker,' he claimed loudly. 'So you want to be a plumber's mate sonny?'

I felt like Oliver Twist asking for more as he walked around me, looking me up and down.

'Yes Sir,' as my mum told me to say.

'Don't call me Sir, call me Tom,' which made me feel a bit better, and we continued to chat about what he wanted from me.

'Is that bike you have there reliable?' he asked.

'Yes, I made it up myself,' but I think that was the wrong answer. He said I would have to save up for a new one when I started getting wages as I might have to cycle to different places each day to meet him.

As we were talking in his garage office his wife came in with a tray of tea and biscuits, and introduced herself. They had a quiet chat in the corner of the garage and then Tom turned.

'We will give you a go, but you must think about what I said about the bike. Oh by the way, have you ever been in trouble with the police for anything such as stealing?'

My obvious reply to his question was 'no', which was accurate, but deep in my thoughts hid a secret that I've kept to myself to this very day for fear of the police or my parents finding out. It was December, two years before the conversation. My mum had sent me to Woolworth's to buy a pack of six Christmas candles one Saturday morning. The store was packed and it took ages before anyone could get served, but all the shop girl had to do was to take the money. Despite being hard up and 'rough and ready', to coin a phrase, my mother always taught me to be polite and well mannered. I stood there for ages with the candles stretched out in my hand to the shop assistant, while grown ups were talking over me and pushing in. I became angry and beckoned the assistant to take my money.

'Wait your turn like everyone else,' the assistant snapped at me.

She made me really cross, so I lowered my hand and placed the box of candles into my trouser pocket whilst I pushed my way slowly through the crowded store towards the exit. I imagined someone was chasing me so I ran all the way down Zetland Road, promising myself that it was something I would never do again, and I never did.

I tried to put it behind me but knew in my thoughts it was a blatant case of shoplifting and it was serious, regardless of the items being trivial and of such little value. I guess my answer to Tom Parker was okay in a way, and I thought I would never mention it to anyone. I had started a new chapter in my life in so many ways, and was now starting my first real job.

My job gave me a new way and new friends, and I felt really secure for the first time in my life. Things looked just great all around, that is until I unexpectedly arrived home that afternoon from my interview. I was so excited and looked forward to telling my mum that I had got the job and would soon be bringing home some housekeeping money to her.

Children under 21 weren't allowed to have door keys in those days, so I wasn't able to get into the house whenever I wanted to. I knocked on the door and my father answered.

'You can't come in, we've got someone here,' he shouted, and slammed the door in my face.

My brothers and I had overcome the key situation by always leaving the ground floor toilet window unlatched at the back of the house. I made my way down the back lane along the lower railway bank, remembering it was there where my father gave me the beating of my life. I crept up the garden, passing the shed where I hid my tin of pennies. As I crept nearer to the toilet window I was trembling with the thought of being caught by my father. All of a sudden an express train screamed by, travelling through the busy station and putting me even more on edge.

Under the bathroom window ledge we had an old rabbit hutch that could be stood on from which I could just reach the window to climb in. Luckily for me the window was unlatched. I gently opened the window, from where I could hear several voices. All of a sudden someone came into the toilet, which caused me to move very sharply and fall off the rabbit hutch. Whoever it was, left the toilet door open and I could hear everything that was being said, but I wasn't able to make any sense of it. I sat on the back step for a while until my sister Hilda let me in.

'Here he is Dad, out the back.'

With that I thought I must be in trouble and I entered the kitchen. Everyone was a bit subdued, especially my mum who was in tears. I was longing to tell my mum about my job, but I could see by her face now was not the right time. I wanted to ask her about the visitors but with the look on my father's face I decided not to chance it.

He rarely went to the pub these days but whatever happened today he decided to go, leaving mum, my sister Hilda and me together in the house, which gave me an opportunity to find out what was going on. I asked my mum what the problem was, only to bring her to tears again.

'Nothing for you to worry about,' she sobbed, holding my hand tightly.

To this day I don't like to see anyone crying, especially my mum.

'What are we going to do?' she again cried out.

'Do about what Mum? Please tell me.'

'Make a cup of tea and I'll make you a nice beef dripping sandwich. I haven't prepared any dinner today and I know it's your favourite,' she replied.

After an hour or so mum had cheered up a little and started telling me about the visitors she had during the day. Apparently they were the actual owners of our house who had moved abroad during the war, but now wanted to move back to this country. They were kind enough to give us six months' notice, but my parents had no idea where we would move to. For a while, I just sat there thinking the worst: we had been here before. I lay awake for hours that night thinking about the old cottage we had squatted in. and how I was dragged down the stairs to be taken to the convent as the bombs were falling around us.

The next morning I wanted to tell everyone about my job, but I decided that in view of what had happened no one would really be interested other than Dr. Packer and Mr. Robinson. I had to tell Mr. Robinson first as it meant that I could no longer help him with the milk round on a weekend as anyone in the building trade worked on a Saturday morning in those days. It had been great working with him and making friends with all his customers. In fact I could remember what each customer had each day without even looking at his book. The paper job would have to be given up too as I could no longer fit that in with the hours I was going to be working.

Life was to rapidly change for me in so many ways as the following week I was to start my first full time job as a plumber's mate. Tom Parker turned out to be a very stern sort of employer, which only did me good. He helped me to improve my way of life so much, having a similar influence to Mr. Packer and Mr. Robinson.

Now, with my new employer and friends, my way of life changed dramatically. I became much more confident. The only doubts left lurking in my mind were the thoughts of what the final outcome would be concerning my home, and this tormented me the most.

10

The Final Torment

I knew it was inevitable that our life at home would again be disrupted in the near future, but I carried on with hope regardless of this thought.

For the first month or so, Tom appeared to be very pleased with me and my work, and he taught me so much more than just plumbing, Tom's pride and joy was his car which he used for pleasure and as well as work. Every Sunday, weather permitting, he would have me cleaning and polishing it. In fact over time I was to become a part of his family, sitting down to Sunday lunch with them most weekends. With a tablecloth and proper cutlery, it was wonderful for me as I was not used to this luxury.

One day the inevitable happened, as Tom had feared it would, when my old bike let me down and I was unable to travel to an important job, losing half a day's work. He was not amused and he deducted my pay.

'I hope that's done something to teach you a lesson,' he said, and he suggested I took his advice and bought a new bike.

Back in the 1940's new bikes started at about £21, which was more than I could afford at the time. Tom suggested that I should buy one to pay in instalments, but my dad would not sign an agreement for hire purchase due to his situation. In the end Tom paid the deposit and signed the agreement for me, making me promise to keep up the monthly payments. I picked up my new bike, which was called a 'Mercury', the following Saturday afternoon from a shop at the top of Pigsty Hill in Bristol. It was blue and very sporty, with dropped handlebars: I loved it very much.

As the weeks passed by I spent very little time at home and more time at my place of work, including weekends. I was hardly at home apart from sleeping. I felt my way of life was changing for the better, but when at home I still sensed a pending disaster that I was sure would descend on us all yet again. In a way, I think I was trying to escape before it happened. When I did go home, Mum would greet me with, 'Hello stranger, nice to see you'. She meant well, but she did make me feel a bit guilty.

One day, I decided to pick up the money I had left in my money box in the shed and noticed the garden I had kept so lovely had since gone to ruin, which was another sign of the deterioration in the home.

While there, I crawled into the chicken shed where over the years I had hidden so often from my dad, many times when he had been drinking heavily. The chickens were all gone now but while sitting there in the deep straw, which still smelt of poultry. I remembered my favourite cockerel called Henry. We all loved him as a pet, but one day, unaware to us children, dad had wrung his neck and my mum served him up for dinner. We didn't have a clue and we weren't told until much later that day. We all cried when we found out that we had eaten him.

I sat in the shed for quite a long time as I was more comfortable there rather than in the house. The rain had started falling on the galvanised roof, making me feel so secure. With the sound of the express trains screaming by I thought of the rubbish tip just down the line where we had spent so many wonderful sunny days making our pennies. Sadly, we would never walk that route together again. I remembered the security man we used to hide from at the tip and the armed soldiers patrolling the lines during the war. We even climbed under coal trucks while they were being shunted: what nerve we had. I felt really quite choked, but I think my emotion was more to do with the thought of where we might be in the next six months.

Four months on I was well into my job and I was doing very well, apart from plumbing, Tom was teaching me most things in the building trade and he started to leave me on my own with some jobs. I did however make my first mistake by cracking a toilet pan while fitting it, which Tom was quite annoyed about.

'If you did the job the way I told you, it would not have happened.' He was correct. I thought I knew it all.

Perhaps with the chapel and my new job, maybe I did get a bit too sure of myself, as my father was to point out to me in a very accusing way during one of my rare evenings that I stayed in. Since the beating I had from my father years ago he rarely showed me any anger, but on one Friday evening he saw me giving my mum some money from my wage packet. I could see he was getting agitated as he started saying things just trying to get into an argument

Because of my regular attendance at my chapel I had learnt to let aggression go over my head. This seemed to annoy him but that was never my intention.

'I think it's time you came down from your ivory tower,' he shouted at me. 'You are too big for your boots and I think you had better stop working for Tom Parker as he is a bad influence on you.'

I wanted to talk about it but I feared another hiding so started to leave the room.

'I haven't finished yet!' he shouted. 'Come back here. Regarding your Mr. Parker, who gave him permission to forge my name so that you could buy that bike?'

My dad had some idea that only parents could sign hire purchase agreements regarding their family. He was wrong, but I was afraid to tell him so, and the very idea of me giving up my job was crazy as it was a wonderful start for me in every way. My father stood in front of me waiting for an answer, but in fear I never said a word.

Suddenly my mother got out of her chair and stood between us shouting, 'That's enough Bill, leave him alone.' In the past he would have punched her for that, but he didn't, he just sat down and said no more.

With this latest attack on me, and thinking about the pending development regarding our home, for the second time in my life I though about leaving home and finding lodgings. All the time I knew my poor mum would be the first to suffer, but I was unsure how much more of this I could cope with. The next day was a Sunday and it was time for chapel again. I decided to go to the old church in the morning as well as the chapel in the evening. I was so happy and I volunteered to help with all sorts just so I could be there.

Two weeks later, Billy Graham came to Bristol on a crusade and I attended several meetings. I can't describe how wonderful I felt. It was like being a part of another life and made me forget the torment at home. Whatever he stood for, he just produced a feeling of wellbeing inside me. It was only when I was on my way home from chapel that I felt desperation and fear. I can recall peering through the front privet hedge one evening in the pouring rain. I was looking into the house for some sort of calmness, fearing I might have done something wrong.

Nothing was mentioned at home regarding our destiny for some time, but when I returned home from work one Friday I had the shock of my life as again I came home to an empty house. In fact it wasn't just empty, it was locked up as if we had never been there. I ran down the road in tears and around the short lane to the back of the house and to the toilet window that my brothers and I had left unlocked so many times before. The rabbit hutch had even been removed, and I could see that the window was securely locked.

I crawled into my secret part of the chicken shed which still remained standing. While lying there with some of Henry's feathers stuck to my trousers I burst into tears and called out for my mum, something I was to do in later life when I nearly drowned whilst in Australia.

I sat there for some time thinking about the squat in Tockington where all this had happened before and started wondering where my family was yet again. Not a word had been said to me that morning, and I have never understood why to this day.

Suddenly, I heard Alan talking to his mum in the back garden next door as he helped her take the washing in. I scrambled out from the shed as quick as I could, calling his name. I was so pleased to see him, hoping he might know where my mum had gone.

'What has happened here today Alan? Do you know where my mum is?'

'They have moved to Hambrook,' his mother answered, but she didn't know exactly where.

They both looked at me as though they knew much more than they were willing to tell me. They went back in the house slamming the door behind them, not wanting to become involved.

I still had a key to the small shed where I kept the gardening tools. To my surprise I found it to be untouched with the padlock intact, I unlocked it and looked inside to find the old wooden wheelbarrow which belonged to my grandfather as well as the aged collection of tools which I cherished so much, still just as I had left them. The big spider that had been there for months was still crawling around as though he knew I was there. If it were my brothers there, they would have killed it by now.

As I walked to the bottom of the garden, closing the gate behind me, I noticed two remaining bikes that Ken and I had built. The railway bank I had set fire to all those years ago had replenished itself with spiky shrubs and lovely yellow flowers. This like the house would be a place where I would never walk again. I returned to the front of the house where Mr. and Mrs. Wainright came out to speak to me. They were in their eighties and were always lovely neighbours. How they put up with all of us for all those years I will never know. They too had no idea what had happened that day or where my family had gone. They just wished me well. Mr. Wainrite shook my hand in a grown up way which made me feel quite important, but my fears soon returned as I made my way up towards Ken's house, hoping there might be a message for me.

I took the shortcut down the back lane passing the old pig bins. Finding one tipped over, possibly by a dog or fox, reminded me of how people would scavenge them for any bits of vegetable waste during the war.

Thankfully, Ken's mum was at home. She noticed my distress immediately and put her arms around me straight away. For years I seemed to spend so much of my time in tears: how much more was I to endure?

No message had been left as I had expected, but as always,

Ken's mum and dad made me feel welcome and let me stay the night. I had to be in work the next morning so was up and on my bike very early. How I got through that morning I will never know as I never even told Tom Parker what had happened. I rushed back to Ken's straight after work to find that my mum had been there that morning looking for me and she had left details of where they were. The details didn't make any sense to me, I knew the area so well, and I knew there were no houses around there.

The details my mum left me said I should cycle up the Hambrook Road at about 1pm where she would be looking out for me. Still very confused, I did as she had written and to my terrible shock I eventually found her standing outside the Polish camp where I had stood so many times before during the war, hoping to get something to eat passed through the barbed wire.

'Where do we go now, Mum,' I asked. 'Where are we living?'

'This is it,' she said.

'I don't understand. Why are we here?'

'Just do as you are told and follow me,' she shouted as we passed through the big steel gates.

I was expecting to see the Polish soldiers marching around and passing the time of day writing their letters home. I was quite familiar with the layout of the camp and as we passed by a number of the wooden barracks I noticed the old cookhouse where many hot meat pies had once been smuggled out to me and my friends by the soldiers. I'm sure I could still smell the pies, as I could still smell the cottage pie I had at the convent at Weston Super Mare, which seemed a lifetime ago.

As we turned the corner I saw my sister Hilda standing in the doorway of a barrack room on the corner of the square. She waved but I was too ashamed to wave back. During the last year or so I had grown up such a lot, and I felt I had become used to something much better. There were about five steps leading into the hut, taking it to about three feet off the ground. It was very cold inside and the bare boards creaked with every step. I just wanted to turn around and run for my life.

Mum led me into a small room at the end of the hut and said I could have it for my bedroom if I wanted. I reluctantly said yes but secretly had no intention of staying there any longer than I had to. Now I was employed, I knew that I could afford some lodgings of my own. That Saturday night was the only night I intended to stay there. It was one of the coldest nights I could ever remember, and I was so cold I could write my name on the inside of the frozen windows.

The soldiers had left many drawings and messages on the wall. We couldn't read them as they were written in Polish, but I'm sure some were quite personal and important to them; possibly some of them might have even been rude ones. There was a bundle of letters I found which had fallen behind a loose plaster panel, perhaps intentionally but had been forgotten. I gave them to mum but don't know what ever happened to them. Today, in the era of computers, finding something like that would have been so exciting. It may even have been possible to trace the descendants of the original owner of the letters.

The next morning I was up early before any of my family were awake and ventured outside to a lovely but cold morning. Looking around I realised that there were other families who had been there for quite sometime. I didn't wash that morning as although I understood there was some sort of shower area which had been used by the Polish soldiers, I didn't know where it was. It was a Saturday, which of course was chapel day, and by that evening I needed to wash and tidy up somehow.

Ken's mum always told me to go there anytime if I wanted a bath, so that day I did. She was eager to know I was alright in view of what had happened. When I told her where I had ended up she was shocked and offered me lodgings if I wanted to live with them. I would have loved to, but I knew my dad would have dragged me back as he had done before.

After having my bath and enjoying a Sunday lunch, I realised that the clothes I was wearing were not quite smart enough for chapel so reluctantly I cycled back to the Polish camp to change. I was still, even at that age, determined to call it a camp and not my home, which I think annoyed my family, especially my dad. I can remember my sister Hilda's boyfriend who was in the Merchant Navy on leave and called in to see her. I was so embarrassed for her.

I think I was waking up to reality, not getting too big for my boots as my dad kept telling me, so I continued to keep my head down and spent as little time there as possible. As time passed, I was to spend much more of it with my chapel friends and attending the little church in Filton, which I loved so much with its early memories. The chapel now had a lovely organ which had replaced Mr. Robinson playing his saw. High up in the apex of the church, I could still see some of the big cobwebs that we could never get to, They seemed to be so beautiful now as the rays of sunshine shone through the tiny dusty window at the top.

Despite my feelings about the camp, and the fact I had no intention of staying there, I made the best of my room. I even used the hiding place in the wall where I had found the soldiers letters to hide my money and private things. The soldier had possibly used this to hide his ration of cigarettes as I found many remnants. There were many Bible texts that I was very fond of, so I pinned them to the walls of my room along with a picture of Billy Graham, but this was the beginning of the end to my father. One Sunday evening, arriving home from evening service, he was waiting for me and dragged me into my room, where he had torn everything off the walls.

'Next Sunday you can stay home with your mother and give up this nonsense once and for all!' My old fears of my terrible beatings returned and I thought it was going to happen again, but he left the room without raising his hands, much to mum's relief. I never said a word but in my heart I would never give up my Sundays and the church, as my life had changed for the better in so many ways and I had made so many good friends there.

At this present day of writing I have just driven to the very house we lived in before moving to the camp. Seeing it again took me back to such clear memories that I wanted to knock on the door and tell whoever lived there now all about them. With all the work done on it over the years, the house looked almost new as if it had no history. The lane on the side no longer existed and the fields where we played and made dens during those long hot summer days had gone forever. My wife was sitting next to me: I don't think she noticed the tear running down my cheek.

The former camp area is now covered by supermarkets and suchlike and you can't tell it ever existed. Just over the hill now stands Filton College, and opposite is the graveyard where my parents lie. With them is my brother Ron, and most tragic of all, my dear youngest sister Jenny, who in a strange way may have saved my life during a terrible ordeal - but I will come to that later in my writings.

The night dad ripped my things off the wall I made up my mind to leave the camp one way or another, and I did on a number of occasions, only to be dragged back there by my father. My mistake was to stay with local friends, making it easy for him to find me. Finally, through someone at my workplace, I was told about some lodgings in Bristol that were vacant. They weren't too expensive and only fifteen minutes by cycle to Tom Parkers house. Over a few days I gradually managed to move all my belongings to Tom Parker's garage without any of my family noticing, and I was ready for my move to Bristol.

I remember that Monday morning I left the camp so secretly and left some of my clothes behind so that mum would not suspect anything. I gave her a cuddle saying, 'sorry Mum' under my breath, which was not normal practice for me as my mum was a very private person and found that kind of attention embarrassing. I on the other hand call it love. Sadly there are so many people in this world who will never really know what love is but to this day I will never understand why. What's more wonderful than being held or holding someone you love?

11

Gaslight

That morning I finally made the break and moved to Bristol, into lodgings in Horfield belonging to a Mrs. McBerty. My father had no idea where I had gone. He did turn up at Tom Parker's house several times but eventually gave up when Tom threatened to call the police.

At last my father was out of my life forever and it was a few years before I ever saw him again. In that time he was to have a further three children, but I had little knowledge of this for a number of years.

For the first time in my life I had really left home, even though it was less than ten miles from Hambrook. As I approached my new home after work that Monday I noticed the rebuilding work that was still going on from the wartime bombing. The houses looked so drab with heavy smoke coming from most of the chimneys blocking out the sun. There were very few cars around compared to today as only the well off had them. I noticed an old man with a distinctly bent back delivering logs as his horse chewed away at a meal in the horse bag while standing on the cobbled street. By the aroma of manure I detected the horse had just 'done its business'. I was quite expecting someone to run into the street with a bucket and shovel to use it on tomato plants which was common practice in those days. I was to get to know old Tom and his horse Flossy quite well over the next few months as he was to deliver to Mrs. McBerty quite regularly.

Halfway down the road I opened the creaking gate and made my way to the front door. I was surprised it had a steel gate as most had been melted down in the war effort. The terraced house, like all the rest, had a large bay window and inside I could see a giant aspidistra plant sitting in a huge glazed pot, partly hidden by thick green velvet curtains hung around the bay window. It reminded me so much of my gran's house in St Paul's where I had spent many happy Saturdays over the years. I was a bit nervous but I eventually knocked on the door using the huge polished lion door knocker moulded from brass: I didn't know what to expect.

I waited two or three minutes for the door to be opened, but it seemed like forever. I wanted to walk away but was distracted by old Tom urging Floss to move on. As I turned back to face the door again it opened about four inches and suddenly a grey haired old lady peeped through the gap.

'Yes, Who are you?' she shouted abruptly in a strong Irish accent.

'My name is Keith, and I have come about the vacancy for a lodger.'

With that she opened the door fully. She was wearing a long black dress to her ankles and navy blue 'daps', or plimsolls as they might be called today. Her long silver grey hair was tied around the back of her head and somehow returned to a small bun at the back.

I wasn't sure about the age of the house, but once inside I immediately noticed the drab wallpaper and worn woodwork: it looked as though the place had not been decorated for at least fifty years. The thing I noticed most was a very strong smell of stale gas coming down the long dark hallway which lead to the scullery. As I followed her down the hallway to the parlour her shape seemed so large that she blocked out the light as we passed through.

'Sit yourself down so we can have a chat and a cup of tea,' she said.

The kettle was already boiling on a parlour range that was identical to my gran's, which again brought back happy memories. It was fairly dark in the room and I automatically looked for a light switch only to discover the house had no electricity but was still gas lit, which accounted for the smell of stale gas.

Suddenly, Mrs. McBerty returned from the scullery with a plate of bread and jam saying that the tea would be ready soon. By then I was getting quite hungry and anything would have done.

'Well,' she said. 'I charge £2-10 shillings per week, which includes your meals and sandwiches for work but it will be 'maggie' on your bread and not butter as it is too expensive,' maggie being margarine.

The time moved on so quickly. Before I knew it the time was 6.45pm at which point Mrs. McBerty turned on the radio to listen to Dick Barton Special Agent, a favourite radio programme for so many listeners in that era.

As the evening progressed it became quite dark in the room and for the first time I was to see the igniting of gas mantles, which looked like a fine gauze type bulb. They were extremely fragile, hanging on a flimsy unit suspended from the ceiling. I had seen the old lamplighters on the street with their long poles doing the same thing, but had never seen it in a house before.

After we had our tea, and listened to her radio programme, she showed me the rest of the house that by then had become quite dark. I followed her into the tiny scullery where she lit a candlestick saying it was for me. I followed her up the dark staircase and realised there was no lighting at all, hence the candle. The stairs were covered in a worn out blue Victorian carpet, the landing and bedrooms had no floor covering whatsoever.

'Well Ken, if you decide to stay, this will be your room and your bed if you want it.' She never did stop calling me Ken the whole time I lived there, but I never really minded.

She continued to tell me that I had to wash in the scullery, which only had cold water, and that the toilet was in the back yard. I was a bit undecided but thought of my reasons for leaving home and so I said yes.

Most of my belongings were still at Tom Parker's, but being so late I made the best of what I had that night. I noticed the lack of pillow cases as I lay my head down on the old grey pillows patterned with black stripes which was very common in those days, but at least it was clean.

As I lay there, the candle flickered light across the bedroom creating all sorts of shapes in the dark corners. I pulled the thick Witney blanket up to my ears. I felt secure and free, at last.

'Don't forget to blow the candle out Ken,' she shouted at the foot of the stairs, somehow making me feel at home.

Looking back on my life I think how unclean I must have been through my basic living conditions, but that was the same for so many other families in that era. I must confess that I found it very difficult to cope with everyday hygiene at Oak Road, but fortunately I was able to make good use of the local public swimming pool in Gloucester Road where I could get a hot bath for as little as three pence.

I remember hating the thought of going downstairs to the outside toilet at night during the winter months. It had many large spiders crawling around, and the inevitable torn up newspapers on a string. Even at home we had managed somehow to acquire proper toilet paper.

12

The Ultimate Shock

After a month or so in my new home I finally settled in and got to know Mrs. McBerty much better. She loved to chat about her past and the old Bristol as she knew it, and I had a great deal to tell her too which was to reveal a most interesting story about my father's mother. Apparently, my gran had owned and run a corner shop in Oak Road many years before with her son, my uncle Clifford. He had volunteered to join the army where shockingly he was tortured and killed by the Japanese. Mrs. McBerty knew them quite well and even said she could see a likeness to Clifford in me.

Until that conversation with Mrs. McBerty, I had very little knowledge of my dad's family including the fact that when my dad had been in the army, he had been stationed in the Black Forest area in Germany. All I could remember was him being in the Home Guard in later years. It was so uncanny that I should move to this street where my family had past connections: I had no idea whatsoever.

As time passed, my life got back to some normality. I was getting on with my job and I was back with my friends at the chapel. I saw very little of my friend Ken as our interests were quite different, but I never forgot the wonderful days we had together earning our pennies with the old bikes, jam jars and apple scrumping.

I was still wearing some of the clothes that Doctor Packer gave me but decided it was time to buy some new ones of my own now that I was earning a wage. The first item I bought was a fine blue suit and a pair of light brown shoes costing a total of £8.00. I felt so proud when I next went to church and equally proud when I was with my closest friend Kitty, who always stood by me wherever I was. There was of course a funny side to my shoes because every time I wore them the brown dye from the artificial leather soaked into all my socks and stained them.

Because I was constantly out in the evenings and at weekends my relationship with my landlady started to become difficult as I think she had started to rely on my friendship. It would be especially difficult when I had to work late to finish a job and would arrive home late for my meal, which I did understand in a way.

I never asked her if she had any children but as time went by I felt she looked upon me as a son. She did have this huge tabby tom cat which I knew she spoke to all day long when she was on her own. I could even hear her in the night talking to it as though it were a human being.

There were a few things I could have complained about at times, but I remembered how bad things had been before. However, I was not always happy with my food, such as my sandwiches for work which some days had raw black pudding cut into inch chunks and no margarine. I did however eat them because I was hungry. I always remember my mother's thoughts on wasting food. She would get so angry if we wasted a crust.

Over the previous few difficult years I had learnt, sometimes by chance, many secrets that had been kept from me for whatever reason: what I was about to learn shook the foundation of my very soul.

Quite by accident, I discovered that my brother Bill was living within a short distance from Oak Road, just up the hill in Filton Avenue. I was to see him standing in the front garden of a house near my chapel the following Sunday afternoon. I knocked on the door hoping that I had not made a mistake, fortunately Bill answered it and he was so pleased to see me after such a long time.

'How did you know I was here?' he asked.

'It was just by luck,' I answered.

'My landlady is out at the moment. Come in and have a cup of tea and a fag: of course, you don't smoke do you?'

There was so much to talk about that neither of us knew where to start. We ended up chatting for more than a couple of hours, talking mostly about the reasons why we had left home and what we were now doing with our lives. The subject then came up about mum and how tough it must still be for her. We both knew that we could never return home with dad still there, which was so sad.

'I suppose we should both consider ourselves lucky that we are here today,' said Bill.

'What do you mean?' I said.

I had heard that line said so many times, especially from dad. I remember one day he said that same thing to me twice, making me so angry that I told him I never asked to be born. That earned me a punch in the face.

'What's the big secret Bill?'

'Well, when our mum was having you she was taken ill at home and dad had to run most of the way to Southmead Hospital with mum in his arms. Where finally she gave birth they said you would not survive, and mum should go home after two days, but fortunately you pulled through.'

'But you said we were lucky, so what happened to you then?'

'I promised mum that I would keep it to myself, but I will tell you as I don't think it will matter anymore now that the family seems to be splitting up.'

Bill reluctantly continued to explain that when war broke out, and I was nearly five years old, mum and dad decided to take advantage of a government offer of sending us children to Ontario, Canada for the duration of the War. The intention was that we would all eventually settle there.

Our birth certificates and identity cards were sent in preparation for the ship journey, but nearer the date of departure my father changed his mind for whatever reason or premonition, and cancelled. The only things that did travel were our documents, which were never to be seen again: two days after setting sail the ship was torpedoed by Germans. It sank to the bottom of the ocean along with all the children and crew. As I write this I am feeling very moved and sad at this senseless loss of innocent lives. Some say your life is already mapped out, but I will never understand that theory to this very day.

Being a sensitive person I sat for ages trying to hold back the tears. I had a job to speak for a while but partly understood why it was kept a secret for so long.

It was now evening. Bill and I parted, promising we would not loose touch with each other and that we would meet again soon. We put our arms around each other and said goodbye, which was something the Harris family had difficulty in doing for as long as I could remember.

I hadn't taken my bike with me that day so I walked slowly down Gloucester Road, going over everything I had been told. I kept asking myself what if this had happened, or if that hadn't happened. I realised it was quite pointless as what was done was done.

It had been a long day and I felt quite weary as I stopped to sit on a wall which had been robbed of its metal railings for the war effort: the war seemed such a long time ago. I must have sat there for ages. I remember the old street lamps were flickering away with the lack of maintenance and the occasional double decker bus passing by, mainly empty as it was a Sunday evening. The more I thought about what Bill had told me that afternoon, the more I felt as though I was in some sort of dream, or as we say today, in a time warp.

I was abruptly brought back to normality by a loud tapping sound behind me. I looked around to see an old lady peering through a tiny gap in her curtains indicating with her hand for me to push off which I did, saying sorry.

Being so tired, I decided to go straight to bed when I got back to my lodgings. My landlady made me a mug of hot cocoa and handed me my half burnt candle in its holder from the night before. As I climbed the stairs she repeated the same message as she did every night.

'Don't forget to put the candle out Ken, before you go to sleep.'

'Yes Mrs. McBerty. Goodnight.'

I thought I would drop off straight away but I lay there for ages thinking about what Bill had told me. As the candle flickered across the bedroom I imagined those poor children on the ship who were never seen again. I was brought back to reality by my landlady's cat scratching at my door looking for a warm place for the night.

That night was the first time I had really missed my mum since leaving home. I would have loved a cuddle but that was not to be. I also missed going to the cinema together which we had done so often. We must have seen my favourite film, *It's a Wonderful Life*, at least a dozen times. Something terrible happens to a man called George Bailey in the story. He wished he had never been born and was transported into that situation by his guardian angel. It was a horrific experience, which was how I felt that night, but like him I realised I had been given the gift of life. Later in life I was to nearly drown in Australia. Perhaps even I might have a guardian angel.

I must have dropped off to sleep without putting the candle out as in the morning the candle holder was just a pile of grease. During the night I had the most weird dream. I was crawling around streets completely unknown to me in the pouring rain. I was naked except for a white vest, and so cold as I lay on the cobbled stones. I had been crying out for help for hours but there was nobody around. The strange thing was that no matter how much I tried I was unable to get up. Suddenly I saw my friend Kitty walking along the opposite side of the road, dressed in a lovely white dress, but she completely dissolved as she turned into a gateway. The odd thing was she was at her present age but I must have been about five years old.

I was awoken from my dream by my landlady telling me I would be late for work if I stayed in bed much longer. I didn't even have time for breakfast as I charged down the cobbled street just missing the milkman's float while turning the corner on my bike.

The day ahead was not easy as I didn't want to speak about what I had learnt. I just wanted to get back to my chapel in the evening where I could feel at home and secure. I could hardly wait to tell Doctor Packer about everything. I knew he, as always, would know how I should deal with the shock I experienced. The following Sunday I went back to the little chapel where I had spent so many happy hours. It seemed like a lifetime ago.

13

COPING WITH REALITY

I was becoming angry and very sensitive, instead of being thankful for still being alive. I started swearing and arguing with all and sundry over trivial things and people's attitudes, which was not me at all. Even my boss Tom Parker noticed it and told me to pull my socks up. I was to miss chapel for the next month, I became more distant from the person I had always been, loosing all faith in my fellow man. In the end I hated myself so much.

When I finally realised what kind of man I was becoming I rushed back to my chapel as soon as I could. As I entered the doors that Sunday I felt like the man from 'Pilgrim's Progress' who lost the weight off his back as he got to the top of the hill. I was so relieved to see so many nice people I had come to know so well.

I had a long chat with Doctor Packer after the service. I told him what had happened and my feelings of anger. He explained that I had to learn in life that everyone was not like me, and that I would always come across nasty destructive people, which is the work of the devil. He said with determination and faith I would overcome, and he was right to this day, but it has never been easy for me. Whatever my readers think of my experience and involvement with my chapel, I can only say that they were the happiest days of my life. I wish to this present day that I could be as worthy as I was then.

My days at Oak Road were to become numbered as during an evening out I was to meet a chap whose mother also took in lodgers. He explained how nice their lodgings were and that he would mention me to her. Within days I met his mum who showed me around the house, which was very homely and comfortable. I would be able to have a proper hot bath whenever I wanted, a cooked breakfast every morning, evening meals and a packed lunch tin for work. This sounded like heaven to me so straight away I said, 'yes please Mrs. Brayley'.

I was dreading telling Mrs. McBerty as she did her best, but the hygiene facilities were a little behind the times and I was getting a fed up with the food and being so cold at night. She was a bit upset when I told her as she said she had got used to me and the cat would also miss me if I went. I think she also took in a lodger to help towards her pension which was quite the practice in those difficult times. She asked me to stay for at least two weeks so that she could find another lodger which I agreed but soon regretted. A lodger moved in within three days with a put-u-up bed in the same room as me. Without meaning to be unkind he smelt like old boots and snored all night, keeping me awake. His name was George, and quite a pleasant sort, but I'm sure he kept a bottle of rough cider or something under his mattress as the whole bedroom smelt of it. He had a habit of walking about in the bedroom with nothing on which made me feel a bit uncomfortable. I did feel guilty about deserting Mrs. McBerty as her lodgings had been heaven to me compared to where I had come from, and I never forgot that. However, I also thought about no more cold water washes, no more gas lighting and candles, and no more trips down the garden in the dark - not to speak of the torn up newspapers where I had the occasional read of news from a week before or more.

I gradually moved my belongings to my new lodgings and finally left two weeks later, as I had promised. I remember the day I left quite clearly. Mrs. McBerty was quite upset, refusing to say goodbye as she gazed into her small log fire in her poorly lit lounge. I picked up my bag and I made my way through the long dark hallway to the front door holding the highly polished doorknob for the last time and pulling the door shut behind me.

Two doors down the road the log man was delivering and his horse once again had his head in his feed bag making a noise on the cobbled street as his back legs were jittering here and there. It was so much like the day I had arrived there. Although I was moving on to better things I felt a bit sad as I walked down to the horse to say goodbye. I smoothed him for the last time but he was more interested in his food than me.

With that I moved away on my bike but had to stop on the corner to have the last look down the cobbled street which had been the beginning of a new life for me. It was my short stay there where the most disturbing revelation of my life occurred. I felt quite choked and turned around again for one last look. To my surprise Mrs. McBerty stood at her gate waving like mad and shouting, 'Take care Ken'. That was all I needed to bring me to tears as I waved back and moved away. Although upsetting, I was glad she came to her gate and wished me well. I was still in tears as I cycled down Muller Rd towards my new home.

My life was so busy from then on and I never saw her again but will always remember her as the lady that could never get my name right. Perhaps I should be called Ken as she always said I looked like a Ken. How strange.

....

While writing my story, I realised how much ground I had covered and felt that it was time to explore any of the landmarks in my life that might still remain and had not disappeared with time. I chose a lovely sunny day for my trip and drove first to Tockington, looking for the condemned cottage where I was left on my own at the age of five during the war, eventually to be sent to a convent.

As I approached the village, I looked up the narrow main street to the small island near the village green where my brothers and I had spent many a Sunday playing. We had been so happy even though, like many other children, we were poor and hungry. I could picture the barrage balloon that came down on the green during an air raid, and how we all ran for cover expecting the worst as there seemed to be an explosion of white powder covering most of the green.

Where I pulled up in my car, the old cottage was immediately in front of me and I could feel a strange chill passing through my body as though I was lying on top of that dark landing waiting to be taken away again. One visual memory of the old cottage was of a huge crack that went down the whole front of the stonework with a large 'Condemned. No Trespassing' sign. The cottage is now a pale pink but doesn't look lived in. Each window lacks curtains or even a flower vase. Possibly the same trees as I had known now lean across the whole roof as though they are about to swallow the whole cottage.

Later in life, I was to make great friends with a lady in her eighties who I called my 'Florence Nightingale'. She believed that you could always tell if a house was loved or unloved, which I believe, and this cottage I felt was one of the unloved.

As I moved on from the village I took a last look at the cottage through my rear view mirror and many memories flashed through my mind, both happy and sad. It was only a matter of minutes before I arrived at my next house, down the stone-walled country road where my dad used to carry me on his shoulders so that I could see the cows in the field. I was too young to understand what was going on, and how difficult life was. I was so happy with the life I had in my own innocent way.

As I turned into my old road, nothing seems to have changed apart from the number of cars and the absence of the huge communal water pump we all used to share. Today people meet in all sorts of places but the water pump was a regular meeting place in those days for housewives sharing their gossip as they sat around with their headscarves while putting the world to rights. My old house is now truly loved as it had been completely modernised, with a lovely garden at the side making it difficult for me to believe I had ever lived there with its filthy outside toilet and no running water.

Being a narrow lane, I had to drive down to the bottom to turn, which brought me to the old mill that has been converted into a fine house. I remembered having spent many hot summer days here cooling myself with the splashes from the mill while eating my stolen apples. I sat there for a while listening to silence, which took me back to all those years before.

I then set off for my next house, in Patchway, through the country lanes but with the noise of the M5. I knew where that house should be, but due to the decades of progress I was having great difficulty finding it: even the original road leading to it had disappeared. I asked around but no one had a clue until I spoke to an elderly gentleman who got into his car after asking me to follow him, as he said I would never find it on my own.

He was right, I didn't recognise a thing as I walked down yet another lane towards the last house on the right where my adventures had begun. Sadly again I was looking at a house that was not loved as it is now in need of much attention. All the paintwork was peeling away and the chimney pots leant to one side as though ready to fall.

I wonder what my grandfather would say if he could see it now. It used to be so lovely, especially in summer, with the huge cherry tree branches cascading into the lane and plum and apple trees bending over with the weight of their fruit. Even the dark red ivy that covered the house has now disappeared.

Where had the stream gone that ran alongside the house and where my brothers and I had spent so many hours catching tadpoles and newts in bare feet, attracting the occasional leach sticking to our ankles? Instead of a stream was a very narrow footpath with high block walls either side. I wanted to see the wonderful meadow I had left behind all those years ago but I only found house after house and warehouses as far as I could see. I closed my eyes for a short moment and tried to picture my grandfather running down the meadow to my brothers' den as the Luftwaffe and the RAF were fighting in the skies above. I pictured the rabbits in their dozens as they hopped around early in the morning, some trying to get into my grandfather's garden to feed on his carrots and cabbage. Where had all the birds gone, especially the blackbirds who sang from dawn to dusk sitting in my grandfather's trees with the resident robins that I knew so well, and loved so much?

As I leant on a garden wall I was suddenly brought back to reality by a gentleman asking me if he could help. I explained what I was doing but he showed little interest, and even though he was around my age he knew very little about the history of the area. Perhaps he thought I was some sort of undesirable 'sussing out' his house!

Disappointed as I was, I made my way back up the lane to my car, dodging the dog mess here and there, only to come across a young lady lying on the damp tarmac and blocking the narrow footpath. She was smoking something or other and looked as though she was in another world. I wanted to ask her if she was alright as I stepped over her, but she grunted 'Hello', so I guess she was fine. What's happening to our world I thought?

Signs of the past at my grandfather's house had almost disappeared so I thought I would take a look at Patchway Railway Station, where some evidence should still be there from the day Ron and Bill were machine gunned by the Luftwaffe, leaving holes in the walls of the station. To my shock this had been bulldozed down not too many years ago, but beyond that still lies the tip, still in operation, which I may visit another day.

14

My New Family

My new home in Eastville really felt like home, as for the first time in my life I never went short of anything. I had my own bedroom, hot water and regular baths whenever I wanted them, plus cooked breakfast and hot evening meals after work. My new landlady's name was Edna and her husband was called Bert. After a while she asked me to call her mum, which seemed wonderful - but also strange as my own mother was not too far away. However I did just that, and I was to lodge there for the next three years until my entry into the Royal Air force.

My first night proved to be very restless. I still had Bill's revelation on my mind and I had another horrific dream. This time I was living in a house overlooking the gorge by the Bristol Suspension Bridge, directly facing the cave doors where I spent many a night with my mum and dad as the bombs dropped on us from above. I'm not sure what I was doing there, or who I was living with, but I must have been young at the time and whoever I was with told me to clean the huge sash windows. I remember climbing onto the dark red velvet window seat looking down at the endless gorge below me and trying to reach the top panes. Suddenly, as I started to press on the glass, the whole window sill and frame came away, taking me with it crashing down onto the gorge and finally the road below. I remember screaming out for my mum as I had so many times in my life, at which point I suddenly woke up to find Mrs. Brayley sat on the side of my bed consoling me.

I was to repeat this dream many more times later in life. Thankfully this dream is no longer with me, although I do still see the house in question on the local television news every day.

Over a period of time I explained all about my past to Edna, which somehow brought me even closer to her family for many years to come. I felt satisfied that I had achieved what I wanted: I was free of fear, had people around me that cared, and didn't have to worry what might happen to my family and me day after day. My dad used to say that I was getting too big for my boots, but all I strived for was something different and better.

With the vast change in my life and family situation I also gave up my job with Tom Parker, who I had been working for since leaving school. He had decided to become purely a house builder, which split us up after a brilliant working relationship. I was sorry in a way as Tom and his wife treated me so well, and I had learnt so much about the trade even though he was so strict with me at all times.

Edna's husband was a manager in a construction company, so I joined him. I continued with my chapel, as I had so many friends there, but the longer I worked with my colleagues and all their practical jokes and bad language, chapel became more difficult. Sometimes out of anger I weakened and retaliated as I became foul mouthed too.

As time passed I was to see Bill now and again, but to my shock and purely by chance I also saw my brother Ron one day. While I was repairing some back fencing for Edna, a car reversed into the lane and I recognised it as his. I was pleased to see him at first, but soon realised he had not changed a bit and was still as aggressive as ever.

'Never knew you were here,' he shouted. 'I hear you have a new mum.', Where did he get that from I thought.

'You haven't changed much have you?' I shouted, expecting a punch in the nose. 'You are still a peasant I see.'

'Do you know what a peasant is?' he shouted back in anger. 'It's a farm hand with a sack like gown with a matching hat with straw poking out of his ears.'

'There you are then,' I said laughing.

It was another two years or more before I was to see him again, and even then he seemed to still have some contempt for me when

I went to see mum, dad and my three younger sisters wearing my RAF uniform and feeling so proud.

'Who has straw in his ears now then, being daft enough to get involved with National Service?' Ron shouted as he arrived unexpectedly.

Sadly, he could not understand that it was something I wanted to do so much, again wanting to be different. Even at my first military interview I was asked what part of the army would I like to join, to which I nervously replied that I would prefer to join the RAF and work in the workshops.

As my interviewer explained, 'You have to sign on for five years to acquire that position. Alternatively you look like a pretty fit guy, and I think you might suit a team of chaps we have plans for.'

I took the second option and became a member of The Royal Air Force Physical Training Team, representing the RAF in recruiting drives on television and many other kinds of shows and venues. I felt so proud as we demonstrated in front of the Queen, televised at the Albert Hall in 1954. I wondered if mum and dad might have been watching. Even at my original passing out parade at Padgate I wished they could have been there but this was not to be.

All I can say to my readers is, if you have a close loving and caring family then stick together and just hang on to them as long as possible. I often wonder if the now dead members of my family such as my mum, dad, Bill, Ron and my dear sister Jenny, taken with cancer so early in life, can see me as I regularly visit their graves. Perhaps I'm crazy but I do talk to them in the hope that they can hear me, especially Jenny to whom I gave my bone marrow in hope of being able to save her life at the time. There is a mounted picture of her on her gravestone which I kiss each time I visit and remember my last words to her: 'I love you Jenny Smith', to which she replied, 'I love you Keith Harris'.

Believing they can see and hear me, I wonder if they disapprove of the revelations in my writing, especially my mum and dad. only yesterday I attempted to tidy their grave and a very sharp thorn from a small stray bramble stuck in my thumb as soon as I touched it, making me gasp with pain and wonder if I had gone too far.

In my defence, I feel I have not only told the story of my early life struggles, but also the story of my parents and family too, as well as many thousands of others mainly through those terrible war years.

As I sat by the grave I thought about another strange dream that I had in past, at the time when I had a very pressured management job at Heathrow Airport and the most important thing in my life was my job, which took its toll on my wife. In my dream I was travelling along the M4 near Reading, going home to Wales on a Friday evening, when all of a sudden the tallest and most beautiful angel stood across three lanes of the motorway. It was as tall as the Statue of Liberty and clothed in white, just peering down at me with one hand beckoning me to stop. In my sleep I braked then woke up wondering if that was some sort of a warning, like the painful thorn in my thumb: so strange.

As I left the graveyard I paused at Jenny's grave and spoke to her again, wishing she could really hear me. I will always remember her as a very gentle loving sister, in fact she was so much like my mother. She was very reserved in her way and like myself, loved her garden and the birds. Why does this mostly happen to the nice people of this world?

15

The End at the Beginning

It was time again to try to recover my footsteps and return to Patchway where it all began all those years ago. I started by visiting the local library where I found some information about Patchway and Filton railway stations, but there was very little information regarding the location of the rubbish dump where we earned all our pocket money during those wonderful carefree days.

Everything had changed so much and I lost my bearings completely due to all the new housing estates and office blocks covering the old meadow. I asked so many people including the elderly like myself but no one had a clue about the local history, or even cared. I was determined however and one way or another I would find the tip, stand in the middle of it and lose myself in its secrets.

Although disappointed, I made my way to Conygre Grove, Filton, driving through many streets which each had a story to tell in my life. Conygre House was where my mum would queue for concentrated orange juice and dried egg powder every week during the war years, and Moody's the grocers was where we sold our jam jars and bought our rationed bananas when they were available.

I passed Ken's childhood home on the way, which was another house that looked unloved compared with how it looked in our young days. I glanced to the side where the council pig bins used to be placed, and where we were to take cabbage leaves and half rotten swedes to help with the Sunday dinners.

As I travelled around I felt as if I was in a time warp, expecting to see my street as I had left it all those years ago, with my friends playing 'kick tin' or playing marbles without cars speeding by. I could picture the greengrocer with his old shabby cart, pulled by an equally shabby horse, with only fruit for sale as he called out 'Apples a pound, Plums' while he rang his loud bell to let us know he was around. I never did understand what he was shouting as he never ever mentioned a price.

I wandered around the back lane to my house, and stood by the rear gate on the very spot my father gave me the beating of my life with the buckle end of his army belt. That memory was quite vivid. Everything looked smaller and darker. The bushes and trees I had set fire to once were now higher than the houses as they hung over the lane below and the railway lines above cutting out the sun.

I wanted to force my thoughts back and cut out from my mind what I was now looking at and imagine how it was with the sound of Qualcast mowers on Sunday mornings and the sound of the old 'matchbox trains' shunting coal wagons night and day on the rails above. I looked into my old garden and tried to picture the chicken sheds and the rabbit hutch against the wall, but it had all changed so much.

Feeling so disappointed, I pulled away fearing that my new car would not stay in one piece if I left it parked there any longer. Fortunately, I found my way closer to the railway crossing I was looking for and luckily that structure has not changed. Even the small grass area where we played in our den looked the same. For a moment as I stood there the memories flowed back to the days during the air raids when we used to dive into the dugout den thinking that it would have saved our lives: how innocent we were.

My thoughts were then suddenly disturbed, bringing me back to the present as a diesel train flew past on the track above reminding me again of progress. The last time I saw a train on that line was the old matchbox train busy shunting coal wagons, with the smiling driver finding time to wave as we sat on the fence. I thought that would be the closest I can get to seeing the elusive rubbish tip, so I climbed the tall bank with the stones slipping under my feet, finally reaching the top with its rusty looking lines running towards Avonmouth and Bristol.

I sat on a spare sleeper for a while, looking across one of the remaining fields which hid the tip from view. It was such a fine sunny day, in keeping with my memories of those long lost happy days when we were oblivious to the seriousness of war while crawling through the tip looking for jars and bike parts.

Looking to my right, I could still see our pond where we spent many hot summer days fishing. Its surrounding trees were now fully grown. I though of Brian too who nearly drowned and wondered if he was still with us today. Before returning over the Severn Bridge to my home in Chepstow I stopped to gather my thoughts on a wooden bench overlooking the village of Lower Almondsbury. With its grey stone church and matching grey slate steeple glittering in the sunshine the lower part of the village seemed to have a slight mist covering it like a village in Bavaria.

This particular beauty spot also holds happy memories for me from the age of five, on a family day out. Across the road was a small shop selling lemonade, off-ration sweets and Smith's crisps, with that little blue bag of salt which was sometimes missing. Sad thoughts also came to my mind as I glanced to my left, knowing that beyond those pine trees my older brother Bill lived, worked and died so young and was known as a popular handyman in the village below.

Sometimes I wonder why I am still here and not at the bottom of the ocean. Perhaps they are selfish thoughts on my part, but as I retread my life's footsteps I become more despondent with now and the future: crazy thoughts I know but although times were tough, I sometimes think of life as a dream being able to wake up lying in a cornfield of my bygone days.

As I drove down the A38 through Patchway the following day, on my way to find the tip, I was reminded of so many adventures as I passed the airfield with its huge wide runway, built to take the famous Brabason Aircraft so many years ago. Concord itself was parked nearby, waiting for its final resting place. Even the remains of my RAF camp was still standing.

Further along the railings there are still wartime air raid shelters where my dad once told me that many people had been killed, and that I was to stay away. Being curious of course I disobeyed him and borrowed a three wheeler bike from a friend's garden, without permission, and rode down to see for myself. The only thing I can remember was all the barbed wire covered in torn clothing, and an armed soldier telling me to go home as there could be another air raid. Yes, I did get one of my father's hidings for borrowing the bike, but I suppose I did deserve that one.

After all my research I finally arrived at the tip, feeling almost as if I had come home after being away for a long time. How can a rubbish tip be home to anyone you might ask. Perhaps it was because I spent so much of my youth there, earning pennies and finding food to eat - from crab apples to sugar beet which was meant for the cattle.

Reaching the tip area I discovered how much things had changed, with new factory units taking up at least a third of the area. Further on I was confronted by an elderly gentleman asking me what I was doing on private property. Being about the same age as me, we found out we went to the same school at the same time. We smiled, both thinking we knew each other, and he told me to take care as I carried on. I moved even further down in the direction of the corner pond where we had washed all our jam jars.

As I walked the rough ground, I could still identify certain areas where bottles were buried, especially the old blue hexagon medicine bottles and various shapes which today are collectors items. I have even heard about a rare shaped wine bottle fetching £400, a bit more than a penny a jar.

Reaching the corner of the tip where the railway lines run north and west I sat down for a rest, trying to remember how everything used to be in my time. I guessed the pond below me was buried many feet down after so many years of tipping. The whole place was now a gigantic mess with its shabby temporary buildings, huge lorries thundering by creating stony dust and many more obnoxious smells. The tip I remembered was tidy: how can one have a tidy tip, one might ask, but it was.

Sitting there, feeling a bit disappointed, I again thought that I must learn to accept the fact that things change in time, like it or not. I suddenly remembered the chap I met at the gate who attended the same school, with the teacher who used to stab pupils in the back with her lead pencil and drawing blood, as sometimes as happened to me.

I was brought back to reality with a goods train rumbling by in the direction of Stoke Gifford. Along the same line we used to spend many summer days picking wild strawberries and falling asleep in our favourite haystack. Across the same field I remembered again where we would break off a piece of straw and drink from a running ditch when our Tizer bottle had run out of water. Can you imagine doing that now?

Reluctantly I decided to leave the tip, hoping to speak to my school colleague on the way out, but he was nowhere to be seen. As I approached the A38 again the lights turned red, giving me a few short moments of thought about the Filton runway in front of me, and the hours spent clearing snow in the middle of the night back in my RAF days.

As I have been writing my story, I have felt quite alone in my own way as I think I have for most of my life so far. I have been looking for something different but can't quite describe what that is. Perhaps it is the same for many people: I don't know.

The wonderful story of Jonathan Livingston Seagull touches my heart profoundly, and in a way I relate myself to the same thoughts and ambitions. Many laugh and scoff at my efforts to write my story, thinking that it was not possible that an insignificant person like me would have anything interesting to write about, but it is the truth and it's something I had to do. My oldest son Michael introduced me to the story many years ago which I have never forgotten and will always cherish. Jonathan's theory was that you have the freedom to be yourself, your true self, here and now, and nothing can stand in your way. This timeless tale will open your heart to wonder and dare you to dream.

Crossing over the Severn Bridge early one morning, playing my Jonathan Livingstone Seagull music quite loud, the bridge seemed to go on forever. So many things in my life flashed through my mind as I glanced down on a view which my brother Bill loved so much, and then to my left where I nearly drowned at the age of four. The remains of the old wooden ferry landing platform where we crossed a few times with my first car was still standing, but its timbers seem to be slipping below the water line.

The following week I was troubled by the fact that I had not achieved my dream of finally completing the journey to where my life really started. I was so disappointed as I felt that my footsteps were in limbo and unable to complete my story. I decided to return to Filton Avenue and look again at my chapel, only to discover to my delight that it was still in operation and with a large congregation. On the way back I decided to stop alongside the fence leading to my old RAF camp.

As I stood there like a child, holding the iron rails, tears came to my eyes as I thought of the times when Ken, Brian and myself used to stand outside the Polish Camp for hours with our arms through the fence waiting for the cooks to sneak some food out to us to fill our empty bellies: may such times never come again.

Every time I touch any part of my deepest past I become emotional and somehow find it difficult to believe that I was a part of so much hurt and fear. I constantly have a vision of how I looked at the age of five, standing quite near where I am now with the dog fights going on above me, lying in a dirty old ditch with torn trousers and bleeding knee caps. Moving further along the fence I noticed remains of the guardroom with memories of daring activities, making me forget my sad moments.

I was to spend the last six months of my service at RAF Filton where I was running the post office and sports store. One summer day in August, the Station Warrant Officer kicked my post office door open, shouting his head off by enquiring if I had completed my office duties. Being honest I replied, 'Yes sir.'

'Right then Bomber!' he screamed. 'I want you to help those useless articles from the Admin. department to do some kerb whitewashing ready for a visit by an Air Marshall.'

The kerb painting went on for three days. One afternoon, as I worked my way up to the outside toilet, I left my post for a couple of minutes to relieve myself. It seems that the Station Warrant Officer turned up at that very moment, and asked one of my friends where I was.

'Haven't seen him all day sir,' was the reply.

That got me confined to barracks for a week, which was very difficult as Filton was a home posting for me, being so close to my former lodgings. I decided to take advantage of my job and daringly leave the camp each evening, returning each morning by hiding under the mail bags in a small truck that was allocated to me each day, complete with driver. When I think of it now, it reminds me of something out of the Carry On films.

Many called me 'Ragamuffin' when I was young through no fault of my own, which haunted me for years. As a result I always tried to be perfect in my personal presentation, although this was to get me in trouble a number of times such as when I had my polished boots nailed to the floor by my Air Force colleagues! At RAF Filton I was earmarked by a extra keen policeman who was unable to find fault with my uniform and presentation, but the tide was about to turn. During one pay parade I noticed that he was wearing red socks under his gaiters, which were not Air Force issue. That same afternoon he stopped me again, walking in circles around me trying to find fault.

Suddenly he shouted: 'That ring you are wearing is not quite the ticket with your uniform airman.'

'My Air Force girlfriend gave it to me as we are getting married in a few months,' I explained.

Enough is enough I thought, so I bent down and pulled one of his gaiters above his boots revealing his red socks.

'This is not normal issue either is it?'

His face was bright red for a moment which changed into a beaming guilty smile, proclaiming that he had only been pulling my leg for a bit of fun all this time. He never bothered me again. My thoughts of the past suddenly came back to the present, as I stood still holding the black half rusty railings within ten yards of the guardroom with all its memories, good and bad.

As I drove away in the direction of home, I was thinking of the following day when I planned this journey into my past by attending the chapel where it all began. Sunday morning was a particularly lovely day as I drove once again over the Severn Bridge.

All the way I was wondering if there would be anyone there who would remember me, or how much things might have changed. I entered the chapel through the same heavy double doors, a bit worse for wear as though they have not been varnished since I last passed through them some fifty years ago or more.

It was difficult to describe my feelings. With the friendly welcome I was given by everyone there, young and old, I felt as though I had come home after a long journey, and yet also felt I had never been away. I was taken aback by the number of young people in the congregation, especially the young ladies looking so natural with their long hair and very little makeup just as they did during my early days. I suddenly thought of my coat of many colours as I glanced up the stairs where I spent many Sunday bible classes wearing it not aware of its obvious difference.

All the people I used to know had gone, but there were three people there who knew Doctor Packer and wife, and Mr. Robinson is still well remembered through his musical input in the early days, playing his wood saw to assist the congregation with their hymn singing.

After a very enjoyable service I was introduced to the preacher, who knew all about the early days and was fascinated by my history and my reason for being there. He talked about a possible sermon concerning the 'Prodigal Son' in which he would refer to me if I did not mind, I felt quite humbled that someone would want to do that for me.

Driving home many things passed through my mind and I wondered if I could ever revert back to the sort of person I was in those days being very content and happy with my fellow man. I have always had this illusion that everyone should be pleasant to each other, but so many people in my life destroyed that theory, sometimes making me angry and becoming no better than them.

16

The Complete Circle

At the age of seventy-two I am able to retreat to a place of great peace - my allotment overlooking the town of Chepstow. This has been my very own refuge for the last six years, throughout all seasons and regardless of weather. When it's raining I sit on a well-worn armchair in my shed, staring out over the town with a cup of tea, or a glass of wine. All my memories come flashing back when I am here and I have time to think.

Some days I have all the intention of doing so many things but someone has always got the kettle on when I arrive, especially in the summer when neither of us will end up doing a thing. I have even fallen asleep in my greenhouse especially after a glass of wine: there too, I find so much peace.

Some days I can hear the hustle and bustle of the town traffic climbing the busy hill, the occasional train passing through and even an old steam train, which causes much excitement. Not far from me also stands the old Severn Bridge where too I had a place of solitude. I used to lie on top of an old gun turret in the sunshine to see the remnants of the old boat ferry on the Aust side disappearing below the water line.

Throughout my life, for whatever reason, I never had time to see the trees as they say. Now, having all the time in the world has inspired me to write my story. As I watch the crows squabbling in the trees above me, I want to take my reader back to the end of my story where I lived for three years before joining the Royal Air Force.

Living with Mr. and Mrs. Brayley was heaven compared to what I had been used to, with a proper bed of my own with sheets and pillow cases, a hot bath and no longer having to go to bed hungry. All this seemed like a dream but it was real, and all those long nights not knowing where I was and sleeping on bare floorboards was a thing of the past.

The first night I woke up crying, with Mrs. Brayley sat on the side of my bed wondering what was wrong. It took me ages to get back to sleep as I glanced around the decorated bedroom with light peeping through from a streetlamp outside. I could feel the white soft sheets touching my body as I held my pillow case tightly as though someone was going to steal it. I felt clean again.

Life was so wonderful in every way as she cooked me a proper breakfast and sent me to work everyday with lovely sandwiches and a big piece of homemade fruitcake bigger than my hand, as they would say in those days.

One day she said that I didn't have to call her Mrs. Brayley as I could call her Mum. I felt so moved by this and I thought of my own mother, wondering how she would feel if she knew: I called Mrs. Brayley Mum until she died many years later.

After being so happy for the previous three years with Mrs. Brayley, life was about to change yet again when I joined the forces: she was very sad as the time for me to go came nearer. I had become so much a part of their lives and they had become so much a part of mine too, which I shall never forget.

After my two years away Mrs. Brayley became a big part of my married life too, being called Nanny by my own children, with plenty of fun and even some tears. At that period in my life I felt that I had won my battle over the war and overcome the hunger, hurt and fear of the unknown. I hope that history never repeats its self again. God bless us all.

Thank you to Cathy and Karen, tutors at Boverton House, Chepstow, who patiently taught me the basics that made this book possible.